In Defence of High Culture

Other books in this series:

Democratic Education in a Multicultural State
Yael Tamir

Quality and Education
Christopher Winch

Illusory Freedoms: Liberalism, Education and the Market
Ruth Jonathan

The Limits of Educational Assessment
Andrew Davis

Values, Virtues and Violence: Education and the Public Understanding of Morality
Graham Haydon

Enquiries at the Interface
Nigel Blake and Paul Standish

In Defence of High Culture

by
John Gingell and
Ed Brandon

Copyright © Blackwell Publishers 2001

ISBN 0-631-22309-6

First published in 2000

Blackwell Publishers Ltd
108 Cowley Road
Oxford OX4 1JF, UK

Blackwell Publishers Inc
350 Main Street
Malden, MA 02148, USA

British Library Cataloguing in Publication Data has been applied for

Library of Congress Cataloging-in-Publication Data has been applied for

Typeset by Dobbie Typesetting

Printed and bound in Great Britain
by MPG Books, Bodmin, Cornwall

This book is printed on acid-free paper

Contents

Foreword   vii

Preface   ix

1. **A Forerunner**   1

2. **Questions of Choice**   17

3. **How to Choose the Best**   49

4. **Popular Culture**   69

5. **How Not to Think About High Culture—
    A Rag-Bag of Examples**   97

6. **The Plurality of Cultures**   117

7. **Practical Implications**   137

Bibliography   145

Index   149

Foreword

There are many reasons why subjects and subject-matter find themselves included in the curriculum. Perhaps they seem likely to contribute to the raising of those mysterious things called 'standards', or to be the source of those no less mysterious transferable skills, or to foster the project of social inclusion. Sometimes of course philosophers of education have argued that a subject discipline is a form of knowledge, one of the ineliminable dimensions of human thought, part perhaps of the Conversation of Mankind [*sic* or not *sic*, to taste]. Politicians have liked to declare in favour of entitlement ('Every child is entitled to become acquainted with his or her literary and historical heritage'), as if they were merely restoring something that their political opponents or progressive teachers had wickedly dashed from the thirsting children's hands. And increasingly if market forces beckon then no further justification appears required. Hence, some may crustily complain, the spread of degrees in all kinds of Studies (Sport, Media, Equestrian); hence too perhaps the endless proliferation of Management and Business programmes as students seek degrees in subjects that will lead to jobs sufficiently well-salaried for them to be able to pay off the debts they accumulated in acquiring the degrees which they studied for in order to, etc.

Suppose, though, that we have put in eveything that meets such criteria as these. Suppose too that we have bolted on every imaginable cross-curricular theme, issue and dimension; to personal, social and health education added life skills and citizenship; to language and literacy added Information and Communication Technology, environmental education for sustainable development, and whatever else is needed to pacify any vociferous lobby that comes along. And, of course, above all there must be learning-how-to-learn, today's universal remedy. Even then—perhaps especially then—one is left with the uncomfortable feeling that something is missing. How, for instance, are Charles Dickens or Shakespeare to justify their place in the curriculum? Or Copernicus, or Charles Darwin? To some, and most notably to Matthew Arnold, it has seemed that such thinkers (or artists, scientists, mathematicians and so on) just are *the best*, intrinsically and in themselves, so that children who never read or study them are deprived of an education worthy of the name.

This is the territory which the authors of this monograph, John Gingell and Ed Brandon, explore and chart in the attempt to determine whether the Arnoldian idea of High Culture can still inspire, still usefully guide us. Theirs is brave cartography, since here be monsters enough—accusations of élitism, snobbery, insensitivity to the multicultural nature of modern socieities—to daunt the enquiring philosopher. For instance, it is complained that the older universities in the UK are inhospitable to the new: to the newer curriculum of higher education as to the newer kind of applicant. They may cease to make *Beowulf* or even Shakespeare compulsory, and have long since ceased to make Latin an entrance requirement, but the culture or Culture which they defend is at heart a bastion of privilege.

Exceptionally, in this millennial year, we are publishing two Special Issues. Gingell and Brandon's analysis of the idea of High Culture is no less timely than this year's other Special Issue, *Enquiries at the Interface: Philosophical Problems of Online Education*. Gingell and Brandon address questions of crucial importance for education in the twenty-first century, and this *Book* is grateful to them for publishing their work in its monograph series.

Richard Smith

Preface

What follows in this book is an attempt to outline a notion of high culture and its role within education. As such, this work locates itself within a modern tradition springing from Matthew Arnold. If the proponents of this tradition had always written cogently, clearly and to the point then the present work would have been unnecessary. Unfortunately the reverse is true. The bearers of this tradition, whilst fighting local battles of varying importance, have dissipated the key insights from which they began and have subordinated the elements of a tradition concerned with reason and value to the winning of Pyrrhic victories. Argument has often been replaced by assertion, reason by prejudice, and a proper concern for value by something which bears all the marks of an empty and pernicious élitism. Because this is so, the authors of this book find themselves in a strange position in that they both want to appeal to the profound insights of the tradition but, at the same time, distance themselves from most of the work produced by those who also seek to place themselves within that tradition. The names of the same cultural warriors appear throughout the book: writers such as Eliot, Leavis, Bantock and Scruton. What follows can be seen as a sustained argument with such writers. But we hope that as an argument it takes none of the short cuts, and indulges in none of the empty rhetoric which we discern in our fellow travellers. Of course, we cannot answer all the problems that our position raises. But we have tried to indicate the directions in which such answers may lie. Whether enough signposts have been provided is for the reader to judge.

This book has been written by two people who share a concern for philosophy, education and fine wine. Unfortunately, beyond this we disagree about almost everything. We hope that such disagreements do not show, or at any rate do not detract from the points we are making. We would like to blame each other for any mistakes we have made, but do not think this is really proper.

Ed Brandon wishes to acknowledge Sharon Gillard for help with word-processing, the University of the West Indies for funding travel to New Orleans and Northampton in prosecution of this project, Ben Schneider's website (http://stoics.com/) for a translation of Cicero's *de Officiis*, and the TPC Fax by Email Project (http://www.tpc.int/faxbyemail.html) which has enabled him to keep in touch with his technology-challenged colleague.

John Gingell wishes to thank Marianne Badharee for typing his contribution, and colleagues in the Philosophy of Education Society of Great Britain for discussions on the topics of this book. We thank Gerald Duckworth & Co Ltd for permission to quote material from Roger Scruton's *An Intelligent Person's Guide to Modern Culture* (1998).

John Gingell and E. P. Brandon

1

A Forerunner

In the course of this book we shall frequently appeal to what we call an Arnoldian filter, a principle we wish to urge for choosing much of what should form part of education in schools. This priniciple is based on a remark in Matthew Arnold's Preface to *Culture and Anarchy*,[1] that culture is a matter of getting *'to know, on all the matters which most concern us, the best which has been thought and said in the world'* (1935, p. 6, emphasis added). Arnold's work here and elsewhere is often seen as a key monument in English humanist thought. Trilling claims that 'he established criticism as an intellectual discipline among the people of two nations and set its best tone' (1949, p. 3). It may not be of merely historical interest to consider some of the concerns that drove Arnold to offer culture in his sense as a contribution to contemporary and future society.

CULTURE

Culture and Anarchy, written at the end of the 1860s, supplies an aetiology of contemporary social sickness and prescribes culture, glossed in a particular way, as the cure. In giving a brief summary of his view, we may adopt Arnold's remark at the beginning of his Preface, in encouraging the Society for the Promotion of Christian Knowledge to republish a tract by Bishop Wilson: 'the reader will leave on one side things which, from the change of time and from the changed point of view which the change of time inevitably brings with it, no longer suit him' (1935, p. 4). Following this, we shall for the most part leave aside Arnold's deep entanglements in religion and the religious controversies of his time, but we cannot avoid noting that for him, however unorthodox his own views may have been, religion with its seriousness and solemnity remained central to social life, and that he thus wished to identify its flourishing with that of culture itself in his understanding of that term.

Arnold sums up his aim in the Preface thus:

> The whole scope of the essay is to recommend culture as the great help out of our present difficulties; culture being a pursuit of our total perfection by means of getting to know, on all the matters which most concern us, the best which has been thought and said in the world; and through this knowledge, turning a

stream of fresh and free thought upon our stock notions and habits, which we now follow staunchly but mechanically, vainly imagining that there is a virtue in following them staunchly which makes up for the mischief of following them mechanically. (1935, p. 6)

Arnold frequently castigated those who imagined that the culture that mattered to him was merely the gentleman's fading memory of Greek and Latin. It is rather a living engagement with our attempts to see the things that matter to us as they are, a study of intelligence and beauty, not for private indulgence but, allied to 'the noble aspiration to leave the world better and happier than we found it' (p. 44), a preliminary to making such ideas and ideals prevail. To study in order to reach a deeper and wider understanding, and to appreciate a wider range of human excellence, was according to Arnold a striving after human perfection, and thus culture converges with the aim of religion as he interpreted it.

While religion comes to the same conclusion as culture, Arnold notes that typically the religious appeal is to a limited, if important, part of human life, the moral. Culture is open to '*all* the voices of human experience'—'art, science, poetry, philosophy, history, as well as religion' (p. 47)—and thus provides a more comprehensive picture of human potentiality. Its lesson is that human perfection is an internal condition, 'the growth and predominance of our humanity proper, as distinguished from our animality' (p. 47). Perfection consists in 'an inward condition of the mind and spirit, not in an outward set of circumstances' (p. 48). It is an endless expansion of human powers, a growing and a becoming.

Culture also teaches that perfection is 'a harmonious expansion of all the powers which make the beauty and worth of human nature, and is not consistent with the over-development of any one power at the expense of the rest' (p. 48). Culture is of great use to us: as *inward* it challenges the place we give to 'mechanical', material and external matters, as *general* it challenges our possessive individualism and as *harmonious* it challenges 'our want of flexibility ... our inaptitude for seeing more than one side of a thing' (p. 49).

Arnold is also emphatic that the concern for culture, for the beautiful and the true, or in Swift's words, for sweetness and light, is not necessarily élitist. The reason he gives contains more wish than fact, but his intention is plain enough: 'Because men are all members of one great whole, and the sympathy which is in human nature will not allow one member to be indifferent to the rest or to have a perfect welfare independent of the rest, the expansion of our humanity, to suit the idea of perfection which culture forms, must be a *general* expansion' (p. 48). He ended his first chapter, the last of his Oxford lectures, with an invocation of equality, reminding us that 'the flowering times for literature and art and the creative power of genius' have been 'when there is a *national* glow of life and thought' (p. 69). But his heroes here, Abelard, Lessing and Herder, offer people genuine culture not, like contemporary churches or the purveyors of popular literature, things 'adapted in the way they think proper for the actual condition of the masses' (p. 69). Culture 'seeks to do away with classes; to make the best that has been thought and known in the world current everywhere' (p. 70).

Whilst culture is potentially limitless in its variety of forms, it is certainly not a matter of doing as one pleases. It presumes standards; judgements of worth are more than an appeal to numbers that can be invoked on one side or another. Arnold disparages Mormonism and its defenders for not recognising the qualitative differences between St Paul and Judge Edmonds (p. 111). Concerning the criticism of literature he remarks on a similar ignorance of the comparative weight of the *Saturday Review* and the *British Banner*.

Part of Arnold's account of the utility of culture is that it results in 'a disinterested play of consciousness upon... stock notions and habits' (p. 211). Much of *Culture and Anarchy* is taken up with examinations of contemporary political issues with this end in mind. Arnold certainly does not speak for a narrow or bourgeois interest in these discussions. As Trilling remarks, Arnold's 'objection to the Real Estate Intestacy Bill is not to what it proposes but what it dare not propose' (1939, p. 286): he raises the question whether private property in land is (still) a real good. In discussing the disestablishment of the Irish Church he likewise makes the quixotic suggestion of establishing the Roman Catholic Church in Ireland.

In *Culture and Anarchy* there is very little explicit suggestion about where to look for sweetness and light. Arnold could take this for granted—his book began as the concluding lecture of his series at Oxford as Professor of Poetry in which he had ranged widely over western literature.[2] We have noted that he mentions as sources of valuable human experience art, science, poetry, philosophy, history and religion. But his own preoccupation is obviously with literature. His earlier discussion of Homer's 'grand style' invokes the sculptor, Phidias, and Michelangelo; but, as Houghton remarks (1957, p. 308), this is hardly surprising in that the terminology comes from the painter Joshua Reynolds. Trilling remarks on Arnold's insensitivity to music (1939, p. 139). But his concern for literature is cosmopolitan. Trilling alludes to his recommending the *Bhagavad Gita* to Clough; his judgement was that contemporary England stood behind at least France and Germany in European literature, and his desiderata for an adequate critic are not unambitious:

One may say, indeed, to those who have to deal with the mass,—so much better disregarded,—of current English literature, that they may at all events endeavour, in dealing with this, to try it, so far as they can, by the standard of the best that is known and thought in the world; one may say, that to get anywhere near this standard, every critic should try and possess one great literature, at least, besides his own; and the more unlike his own, the better. But, after all, the criticism I am really concerned with,—the criticism which alone can much help us for the future, the criticism which, through-out Europe, is at the present day meant, when so much stress is laid on the importance of criticism and the critical spirit,—is a criticism which regards Europe as being, for intellectual and spiritual purposes, one great confederation, bound to a joint action and working to a common result; and whose members have, for their proper outfit, a knowledge of Greek, Roman, and Eastern antiquity, and of one another. ('The Function of Criticism at the Present Time', in Trilling, 1949, pp. 265–266)

While Arnold and his major successors such as Leavis and Bantock have been preoccupied with literature, and education has given pre-eminence to reading and writing, it is our intention to redress the balance in favour of the other elements of high culture, in particular the other fine arts (see Chapter 3 for more discussion). Thus, borrowing from Entwistle (1978), we alter Arnold's phrase to 'the best that has been thought and *done*'.

A crucial element in Arnold's conception of culture is covered by the phrase 'the matters which most concern us'. He shared with Plato's Socrates the belief that ultimately the most important question for us concerns how we should live, what human flourishing amounts to. As we have noted, he admits that science, the controlled but imaginative inquiry into the nature of the universe, is a part of culture; it can make its contribution to seeing things whole. But again like Plato's Socrates, in the end this is for Arnold a small contribution. *Culture and Anarchy* hardly mentions science, and invites the misrepresentation of his views that he elsewhere castigates; a fuller account is offered in his famous reply to T. H. Huxley, the lecture 'Literature and Science'. Here he begins with the thought that traditional literary education was designed for a leisured class and is thus irrelevant to the needs of a world in which most people work in industry, trade or business. Against this he urges that Plato's 'view of education and studies is in the general . . . sound enough, and fitted for all sorts and conditions of men' (in Trilling, 1949, p. 407). Huxley takes Arnold to claim that literature provides sufficient to know ourselves and the world, and denounces the absence of what science has revealed. Arnold replies that humanist study is as 'systematically laid out', as scientific, as physics or biology. He stresses that his conception of literature is not just one of *belles lettres*; knowing ancient Greece is 'knowing her as the giver of Greek art, and the guide to a free and right use of reason and to scientific method, and the founder of our mathematics and physics and astronomy and biology' (p. 412). In studying Rome he mentions law, administration and military matters. And he claims the same goes for modern nations — knowing them means knowing Copernicus, Galileo, Newton and Darwin.

Arnold acknowledges that the process of scientific inquiry is interesting and provides a useful discipline. But to install science as the centre and foundation of the curriculum is, he claims, to overlook the constitution of human nature. Human life is built up by 'the power of conduct, the power of intellect and knowledge, the power of beauty, and the power of social life and manners' (p. 415); nor are these isolated from each other. We want knowledge somehow to be related to the rest of our life, our emotions and our attitudes. Arnold would surely have lost Huxley by the time he invokes Diotima's message for Socrates in Plato's *Symposium* that humans are at bottom motivated by a wish that good should be ever present to them.

Arnold insists that what science offers is restricted to the realm of intellect and knowledge. It has no bearing on conduct or beauty. It cannot connect with our deepest emotional needs. Education however 'lays hold upon us ... by satisfying this demand' (p. 420) that religion and poetry (conduct and beauty) be connected with our knowing. Huxley avers that science has shattered the beliefs that held things together for the medievals. Arnold concedes that it has, but then 'the emotions themselves, and their claim to be engaged and satisfied, will remain' (p. 421); if humane letters engage these then they are even more important when science has destroyed a unified world-view than before.

Towards the end of his lecture Arnold criticises what he regards as the invidious comparison of the value of humane letters compared with that of the natural sciences. He says the scholar of the humanities cannot hope to avoid confronting the lessons of science, but the scholar of science exclusively will know nothing of the 'criticism of life by gifted men, alive and active with extraordinary power at an unusual number of points' (p. 424). Moreover he or she will be tackling a discipline suitable only for specialists. In the main such students will end up unsatisfied and incomplete. If we must choose, then the majority will find greater satisfaction in the humanities: 'Letters will call out their being at more points, will make them live more' (p. 426).

Arnold's explicit position is that we ought not to make people choose, that they should be exposed to both sources of insight. This is, we think, even more pertinent as science and forms of technology imbued with science have become more dominant in our world. It is not obvious that Arnold was right to suppose that a scientific education is suitable only for a minority with an appropriate intellectual bent. Difficult though it is, there is a balance to be struck in teaching science between the aim of mastery for intending specialists and more synoptic but still adequate understanding for the rest. But these issues are not peculiar to the sciences. The fact that our conception of knowledge is now paradigmatically scientific requires that everyone be given a grasp of what this sort of knowledge is like, and of what it can and what it cannot provide (for an account of this, see Brandon, 1987).

Arnold's Platonic view of human nature and its demands leads naturally to his wish to see poetry in effect take the place of religion, to make habitable the disenchanted world of modernity. But we can approach his position without his presuppositions by taking the stance adopted in *Culture and Anarchy* with respect to what Arnold called 'machinery'. There he effectively argued that many things people are inclined to take as ends are themselves at best only means to a particular kind of human flourishing. Arnold cites his contemporaries extolling the virtues of a growing population, or England's reserves of coal, or railroads, or the increase in wealth, or the form of religious organisations or the traditional freedoms of the English, and says that none of these things can be a value in itself. If anything, they only conduce to living a particular sort of life, and that is where value resides. What would more excite the love of mankind, the England of the mid-nineteenth century or that of the first Elizabeth when its coal and industry were hardly developed? 'The aspirations of culture . . . are not satisfied, unless what men say, when they may say what they like, is worth saying—has good in it, and more good than bad' (1935, p. 50). Again health and vigour are important but not things to make a fuss about.

It is clear that many of the items Arnold picked can be disputed. Trilling (1939, pp. 260–265) notes that there is an important difference between Arnold and Mill with respect to the value of liberty and the search for truth, and moreover the right role of state power—we shall comment at greater length on some of this later in this chapter. But Arnold's argument has force: if we accept that values are not some sort of fact discoverable by empirical inquiry then no amount of science or other factual study is going to be able to tell us how to live. What Arnold needs at this point is the reader's motivation even to ask that question, and he might follow Huxley in appealing to the fact that science itself has wrecked most of the religious perspectives that have so far been available to mankind.

ANARCHY

We have sketched, much in Arnold's own words, the picture of culture that he offers. To conclude let us very briefly rehearse his diagnosis of his times. He offers a cultural history of England as part of a wider oscillation in Western civilisation between two complementary but often apparently conflicting forces: Hebraism and Hellenism. Hebraism is pre-eminently a moral concern, its governing idea *strictness of conscience*, and it prevailed too much in English Puritanism. What we required, he thought, was greater stress on Hellenism, which is this-worldly, concerned with beauty and reflective thought, with seeing things as they are; its governing idea is *spontaneity of consciousness*.[3] Alongside these cultural currents Arnold outlines a social or political history in which a large aristocracy that provided a government jealous of the expansion of state power has been overtaken by the power of the middle class, the traditional standard-bearers of Puritanism. This recently arrived middle class is itself facing a growing threat from the working class, to the extent that Arnold anticipated an anarchic breakdown of public order—his book reverberates with the dissensions incident upon the failure of a franchise reform bill in 1866 (see E. Alexander, 1965, pp. 261–266, or the Editor's Introduction to Arnold, 1935).

The decline of the aristocracy was not simply political. In various places Arnold repeats an anecdote of Lord Granville, reciting lines from Homer a few days before he died, as 'exhibiting the English aristocracy at its very height of culture, lofty spirit, and greatness, towards the middle of the last century' ('On Translating Homer' in Trilling, 1949, p. 218). But in *Culture and Anarchy* he calls the aristocracy 'Barbarians' and elsewhere laments: 'if this class had only gone from one source of high culture to another; if only, instead of reading Homer and Cicero, it now read Goethe and Montesquieu— but it does not; it reads *The Times* and the *Agricultural Journal*. And it devotes itself to practical life. And it amuses itself' ('A French Eton', in Sutherland, 1973, p. 156).

The aristocracy might remain serene lovers of beauty but certainly not of intellect. The middle classes, alias the Philistines, were constricted by the narrowness of Puritanism, equally hostile to beauty and the free play of intellect. Arnold anticipates Weber in saying that Puritanism yielded a 'reward, not only in the great worldly prosperity which our obedience . . . has brought us, but also, and far more, in great inward peace and satisfaction' (p. 55) but it was still a cribbed and confined view of human perfection. Its love of liberty and its political system of checks and balances, salutary in a context of feudal oppression, invite anarchy when those restraints are removed. The working class, the Populace, is also found wanting as an embodiment of what culture demands. Arnold is led then to seek to go beyond classes and invoke a Rousseau-like State, 'or organ of our collective best self' (p. 97), as the solution to the conflicts around him.[4]

THE UTILITY OF CULTURE

The defenders of culture have various contributions to make to the enhancement of the social classes. Culture teaches the historicity of social life, and its complexity. It shows that we cannot wipe the slate clean, that not all possibilities are actually feasible at a particular time. For these reasons it tends to be against system and systematisers. 'Culture is always assigning to system-makers and systems a smaller share in the net of human destiny than their friends like' (p. 66).

Culture offers disinterested reflection on what we take for granted. Its best motto is, in Bishop Wilson's words, 'to make reason and the will of God prevail!' (p. 45). Arnold's immediate caution is that we must beware our inclination to act precipitously upon untried preconceptions; culture demands 'worthy notions of reason and the will of God, and does not readily suffer its own crude conceptions to substitute themselves for them' (p. 45). But at least he assumes we can find these worthy notions, that culture has lessons and is not merely a ceaseless search. It offers pictures of what human life might be, and thereby judges. As Arnold suggests (p. 58), to imagine how intolerable Shakespeare or Virgil would have found the Pilgrim Fathers is to say a great deal about the value of the life they carried to the New World.

Culture looks honestly at what human life is, and again judges. People have invoked wealth and religion as measures of success; we have had religion for hundreds of years and what have we children of God done with it? Look at London, with its 'unutterable external hideousness and with its internal canker of *publice egestas, privatim opulentia*[5] ... unequalled in the world' (p. 59). At another level of concern, Arnold notes the reading public gives the largest circulation in England, indeed in the whole world, to the *Daily Telegraph*!

ARNOLD VERSUS MILL

We have alluded to an important difference between Arnold's appeal to culture and the role of criticism and Mill's position in *On Liberty*, a text that lies behind Arnold's discussion. Putting it crudely, it is a distinction between those who think that high culture both offers incisive weapons to undermine current cant and also provides superior answers and those for whom there is perhaps only an unending quest[6] and no final answers.

Mill, conscious of the enormous pressure to conformity of public opinion, even without the concurrence of state power, urged a proliferation of experiments in living, not merely tolerance of those rare individuals who choose to be different. On the other hand, he agreed with Arnold on the supreme educational importance of Greek culture. Mill's rhetoric is captured nicely by Houghton:

> Some of Mill's most living pages are devoted to the right purpose of education: not as at present in the Church, the Universities, and in almost every dissenting community, that the student should become a disciple to carry away 'a particular set of opinions,' but that he 'should go forth determined and qualified to seek truth ardently, vigorously, and disinterestedly'. (1957, p. 286)

But if Mill wants adherence only to second-order logical procedures of reasoning—Socrates' injunction to follow the argument wherever it leads—rather than to any body of substantive thought, one might wonder what is the educational point of the prolonged exposure to what humankind has so far achieved. Arnold's emphasis is different: not only do we need the techniques of criticism, but we equally need exposure to the best that has been thought, to provide exemplars and standards, against which most of what is on offer, and most of what further experiments in living might provide, will be found wanting. Criticism could be learnt and practised on pulp fiction and popular romances, but to hone one's skills on Jane Austen and Stendhal and their portrayals of incompatible yet fully realised types of life provides a richer yield, deeper knowledge of human possibilities as well as critical incisiveness. One could learn the pitfalls of documentation from studying family history and genealogies, or from the more complex and significant events surrounding the beginning of the American revolutionary war.

While Arnold's major concern was with the quality of human life rather than the growth of scientific knowledge, Mill and his more consistent followers have adopted the same view for both, and it may be of some interest, and also somewhat more amenable to summary treatment, to look at the issue primarily in the context of the natural sciences. Lloyd (1997) has recently argued that Feyerabend put Mill's preaching into practice in his defences, against the scientific and philosophical establishment, of astrology and Chinese medicine. He enjoined us not merely to tolerate but to encourage the exploration and proliferation of non-standard positions because, to summarise Lloyd's summary of Mill's epistemological arguments, we are not infallible in our judgement that they are mistaken, they may contain some partial truth, and even if we are in possession of the whole truth on some matter we will not properly grasp it unless challenged to defend it rationally against competitors.

But can we take Feyerabend's injunction at face value? One problem is that philosophers are well aware of varieties of non-standard views that no one would want to take seriously. We have, for instance, the fantasies beloved of epistemologists and sceptics: the universe began five minutes ago; I am a brain in a vat or a Cartesian thinking thing being given impressions as of the world we usually think we inhabit. The point is not to explore these as serious contenders to our normal accounts of things but as stories that hope to reveal various unpluggable gaps in those normal accounts. The potential worry is that we cannot plug other analogous gaps when confronted with serious rival views. Leaving aside high fantasy, the philosophical literature on induction often starts from something like the underdetermination of theory by data: there are countless logically possible variants of the views we currently entertain that are compatible with everything we can come to know. (We might consider infinitesimal adjustments to the values of variables, so small that errors of measurement would never permit us to adjudicate between them, or perturbations localised in impossibly remote galaxies, or grue-like predicates, or other variations.) These again are not being presented as serious candidates for inquiry; rather the philosophical problem is to comprehend on what basis they can be summarily dismissed.

The Millian epistemological arguments for a blanket tolerance are not particularly strong. We may not be infallible judges of the truth, but we are pretty certain that some claims are false. Socrates after all knew that he did not have answers to the questions that irked him, and that involved knowing that what were usually offered as answers were inadequate. Popper, the major fallibilist of our time, rested his position on an asymmetry between verification and falsification, and while a realistic picture of scientific inquiry pushes us some way towards a Quinean holism we are not required to abandon entirely the idea that some such asymmetry remains. So where we can rule out a hypothesis, we can rule it out, and do not need to let Mill's or Feyerabend's argument restrain us.[7]

Again, in some cases we may have good reason to suppose that a non-standard view somehow contains elements of the truth, or at least has some features that bestow staying power upon it, but we are not obliged to think this about all the fantasies we have noted in philosophy. The point that we can only properly grasp a view by seeing it fend off competitors, by knowing what it rules out, has much to be said for it, but again it needs only decent competitors, not the whole range of empirically indistinguishable variants we mentioned above nor the philosophical fantasies. So we might conclude that it is not every non-standard position that deserves encouragement. There is not time enough and space to investigate all the logically possible distinct variants, and many are designed to be empirically indistinguishable anyway, so it is unclear what could be involved in pursuing them.

There are two questions we could now investigate. One is whether there are other non-epistemological arguments for either the original all-inclusive Millian position or some watered-down version. A second is what basis, if any, we can find for the distinction a watered-down position requires between non-standard views that deserve respect and those that can be rejected out of hand (or in the human sphere, between possible experiments in living and insanity).

To begin with a remark on this second issue: we might hope to find an intrinsic, epistemological or at least philosophical characteristic that could do the job. For the sorts of case mentioned in connection with induction, there probably is some such feature to be found, although philosophers have made notoriously little progress with actually specifying the simplicity of theories and related notions. But for the philosophical fantasies, it seems doubtful that we can find anything intrinsic of the right sort to distinguish Russell's five-minute universe from what some people now seriously advocate as 'many worlds' interpretations of quantum mechanics. In any case, we are unable to suggest what it might be. We are led, therefore, to consider merging the two enquiries. We suggest that what is going on here is an appeal to an epistemologically irrelevant social fact in order to choose among non-standard views.

That the idea of *social* endorsement operates can be seen by remarking on an unadvertised move Lloyd makes from encouraging non-standard ideas to encouraging non-standard traditions. One person's belief that Haile Selassie is specially divine may be a sign of lunacy; a sufficient number sharing the belief and you have a religion.[8] Feyerabend could have espoused bits of nonsense of his own devising to provoke the scientific establishment, but it makes things that much more accessible if the nonsense is in the public domain. But we suspect that we have here more than a wish to avoid private reference. The Millian thought that, however odd a view may seem, it may yet have something going for it is much more appealing when applied to views that a number of people have shared than when it is a matter of the views of individuals.[9] One does not need to embrace the whole of Dawkins' meme-theory (1989) to see that views that have been espoused by a number of people and which have therefore presumably played some part in their life, shaping and being shaped by it, should have some sort of fitness to survive, which could be lacking in the idiosyncracies of individuals. But we do not need to embrace the whole of Marx's theory of ideology to see that what gives a set of ideas staying power need have little to do with their furthering the interests of those who espouse them. Nor, of course, need truth have anything to do with it.

These objections undermine an epistemological basis for the suggested criterion. But is it a concern for truth that really underlies the appeal of the Millian line in the sciences? Lloyd argues that Mill was concerned for pluralism in science just as much as in other areas of life, but let us remember that these other areas are parts of the picture and that it is far from clear whether we should even begin to think about them in terms of truth at all. Mill's demand for the tolerance and indeed encouragement of experiments in living can be seen as responding to this fact: that there is no one best way for humans to live. Nor do we need to pretend always to have to choose. We can have Bach and the Beatles, ratatouille and rijstafel. Mill's explicit position, as Lloyd says, is that each individual is the best judge of what he or she finds most congenial. That would lead us, in those areas of human life where we do have to choose one rather than another way of doing things, to move in the direction of some sort of democratic procedure. But again our actual thinking is thoroughly socialised. It is notorious how traditional is our cooking, even when 'revolutionised' by *cuisine minceur* or some other craze. What Mill is in effect and for the most part recommending is letting people choose among the options that groups of people have chosen. We allow ourselves to rule out of court—as insane—some options that an individual might propose, but we respect options hallowed by tradition, ours or that of others. Of course, we do allow some innovation and almost always that is one individual's doing, so we have not yet completely tied down the difference between acceptable and crazy notions, but the point is that we do not in effect treat all proposals equally in the way that Mill's explicit position would appear to enjoin.

The suggestion is then that one feature that might distinguish the non-standard positions to be simply ignored from those that, in obedience to Mill–Feyerabend, we should let blossom is a matter of social contingency: does a group of people subscribe to the position in question? And part of the point of the distinction is that it is not a question of whether one person subscribes to it. We respect a view because it is several people's view. Social endorsement is our protection against individual insanity. And it explains why Mill needs almost as much emphasis on substantive content as Arnold—we need to learn what other people have already tried.

A defender of Arnold's emphasis against what we have presented as Mill's could appeal here to the cumulativeness that we find in the natural sciences. Despite the philosophical puzzles that can be generated, there is an obvious sense in which once Newton has clarified the distinction between weight and mass we are not going to renounce the distinction, however much we refine our conceptions of what the two are in themselves; once we have discovered that water is made up of hydrogen and oxygen in a constant proportion we are not going to abandon that view, whatever changes our detailed account of the nature of atoms may undergo. At the frontiers of physics we can reasonably discuss big bangs with or without 'inflation', we can offer strings in multidimensional space-times as speculative solutions to problems, but no one is going to identify weight and mass or suggest that balls do not accelerate down inclined planes. Where once there were reasonable alternatives, now there are not.

In the realm of conduct, of ways of life, and in aesthetic contexts, it is not so evident that we can give a useful sense to the idea of a *cumulative* build-up of settled opinion. Feasible ways of life, conceived as the way of life of a Greek hero or a samurai or a plantation slave, come and go with social and economic circumstances. On the other hand, the principles or conceptions we might find through which to understand our judgements of their excellence or lack of it are perhaps not difficult to uncover, and have been the common property of reflective people at least since the time they were enunciated by moralists and religious reformers near the dawn of recorded history. And we have found a variety of styles of life that probably suit different temperaments. We have a fair idea of what people would rather not have, though sadly many of them have to put up with these constraints and oppressions for most of the time; and mortality is inescapable for all.

There may have been a deepening and growing sophistication of our commonsensical psychology. Harold Bloom's contention that Shakespeare invented what he calls 'the human', the inwardness of self-characterisation, that 'personality, in our sense, is a Shakespearean invention' (1998, p. 4, and echoes elsewhere), would seem to commit him to some such view, but his belief that Shakespeare plumbed these depths further than anyone since makes this an exceptional kind of case. What we may have here is the aggregation of exemplars of psychological complexity—depth through breadth. This accumulation is not dissimilar to what we find in the arts (and indeed overlaps it): a rough canon, which provides a growing body of standards but which cannot itself answer today's question for us since aesthetic creation demands that its product be for ever new, not a repetition of existing excellence.

Whether or not cumulative build-up is appropriate, Arnold can claim that we do have a range of comparatively platitudinous claims about what makes human life better or worse which it would be idiotic to deny. We suspect that, whether or not his explicit position endorsed it, Mill would have agreed with him, though they might still differ over the extent to which anyone would be justified in interfering with people who choose to follow such idiotic perspectives. We can conclude, then, that there is more to education than merely grasping the second-order tools of rational criticism, and that the substantive achievements of the tradition are an essential component of an informed view of things.

RESPECT FOR BELIEF

To raise a question that will come to the fore in Chapter 6, there is a problem in this vicinity, at least for anyone with the liberal presuppositions of Mill and Arnold. We can see this by looking briefly at one of the more bizarre claims in Locke's work on religious toleration: 'Nobody is born a member of any church; otherwise a man's religion, along with his estate, would descend to him by the law of inheritance from his father and his ancestors; than which nothing more absurd can be imagined' (1968, p. 71). But in fact precisely the opposite is the case. We do not in general find people, in the maturity of their judgement and after careful review of all the alternatives, coming to a decision as to the true religion; they are born into one supposed such. Traditions, of the sort Lloyd invokes, are typically things people are born or inculcated into; they get their hold, not through rational appeal, but through nurturance or Kuhnian propaganda. Such a background often puts serious obstacles in the way of rational thought and action. The examination of reasons for and against is not usually prominent in such upbringing; traditions become deeply entrenched, often impervious to later rational reconsideration. Traditions of these kinds typically give power and authority to some rather than others. Many people are spoken for, rather than left to exercise their own untrammelled judgement.

Respect is due to your opinion if it is an opinion arrived at by the procedures Locke falsely assumes everyone goes through in joining a church (or, more broadly, a religious group). But what are we to say when it is an opinion formed by very different processes, in the absence of Arnold's disinterested play of thought on stock notions?

For one category of person, children, we think we have a right to overwhelm such opinions and replace them with those we ourselves endorse.[10] This is the major task of education on everyone's account of it, whatever else they might suppose. We know that treating grown-ups like children is not conducive to peace and stability, so we refrain from doing so. But is this any more than expediency? If the views have been acquired non-rationally (counter-rationally in many cases), and if we cannot discern in them the seeds of epistemological utility, should our considered opinion regard them as any more than the ravings of a madman? Epistemological anarchism of Feyerabend's kind still needs to supply a grounding for any distinction it might wish to make, or does in practice make, among non-standard ideas. A claim that respect is due to some positions rather than others owes us an account of the basis for that respect when its favoured views are simply those of identifiable groups of people rather than individual idiosyncrasies. Demanding exposure to the best that has been thought and done may not leave mediocrity and obscurantism as viable options; it is a call to conflict, albeit non-violent, rather than peace and love.

NOTES

1. In this chapter page references for quotations from *Culture and Anarchy* will be given to the 1935 reprint of the text as edited by Dover Wilson. Other quotations from Arnold will be referred to from selections of his work edited by Sutherland (1973) or Trilling (1949). The former of these has a text of *Culture and Anarchy* without the Preface. Where several quotations from the same source follow each other, only page numbers will be given.
2. For our present purposes it is worth noting that his lectures had not only invoked the sublime peaks of that tradition but had also advocated obscure writers such as Maurice de Guérin and Joseph Joubert and had included an extensive exploration of Celtic literature and culture—hardly part of the usual canon.
3. Anderson (1962) remarks that seeing things as they are can and should apply equally to our moral life, so that Hebraism can drop out of the picture. Arnold was, however, sketching history, not our basic intellectual requirements.
4. Trilling (1939, pp. 280–284) uses Rousseau and his notion of the general will to interpret Arnold's talk here of our 'best self'.
5. Indigence in public, wealth in private.
6. This phrase is almost the title Popper, in many ways a follower of Mill, took for his autobiography.
7. Qualifications are of course needed. A hypothesis refuted by dubious evidence ought not to be immediately abandoned. If we have nothing to replace it with, we may have to continue to use what we know has been refuted. If we have reason to think that our erroneous view gets close to a better view in most cases that matter to us and is easier to use, we may well continue to use it (as we use Newton rather than Einstein to calculate the mathematics of Shuttle missions). Categories may benefit from redrawing and thus statement forms that are rejected at one time and with one understanding may be reinstated later with a rather different intent. The point is only that we can be more assured in rejecting a claim than in endorsing one.
8. Cf. Walzer's remark that in the USA today 'claims of conscience over a wide range of social issues—the refusal of oaths, of jury service, of public schooling, of taxes; the demand for polygamous marriage, animal sacrifice, ritual drug use, and so on—gain whatever legitimacy they have, even today, because they are religious practices, features in a collective way of life' (1997, p. 69).
9. It is not perhaps irrelevant that the etymon of *idiot* meant a private person amongst the archetypal political animals.
10. Or at least if the ideas are in non-controversial areas. The fact that we will happily correct a child's error in arithmetic but not in religion is another manifestation of the kind of problem addressed here.

2

Questions of Choice

The fact that education is, and must be, a process of enculturation for those being educated gives us some, but by no means enough, guidance as to what we would expect to see going on in our schools. For given that our educational institutions are part of our culture and, given that anything that is part of our culture will transmit cultural messages, if we put children in school and let them play all day, or simply asked teachers to explain their hobbies to the children, then some processes of enculturalisation would be going on. But no one with any real concern for either our children or their education would think such things fulfil a proper role for schools. Certainly if, as Arnold thought, education is a question of passing on, or trying to pass on, the features from our culture that we value, then any such reliance on random processes must be ruled out. Instead we have to select those aspects of our culture which we wish our children to partake of and insist that our educational establishments make sustained and intentional efforts to ensure such participation.

CONCEPTIONS OF CULTURE

The first problem we face concerns the notion of culture itself. It is one of the more slippery terms in the language. There are various ways of using the term and various ways in which one might seek to map out the area it refers to. We shall begin with what one might call the anthropological use. Culture here is:

(1) All the beliefs and practices of a given group or society.

In this sense of the term we can talk about English, Spartan or Azande culture and almost anything that goes on amongst these groups will be relevant to this particular usage. We say 'almost anything' since some things that happen among such people are purely natural events—their hearts circulate blood around their bodies, for instance, or they fall if pushed over cliffs. But once there is a possibility of variation, humans have almost always found ways to select some ways of doing things rather than others, and this is where culture in this wide sense gets an entry. Most of us do not take much thought about breathing, but some groups do for their own purposes, and when we turn to things like eating, drinking, speaking and so on everyone is aware of the cultural differences among such practices. Culture exploits a kind of underdetermination to set norms or standards—we expect people to eat with a knife and fork, while others expect people to use their hands. It gives rise to an important kind of arbitrariness within limits: we must eat, but it is arbitrary whether we use cutlery or our hands or various other methods people have or could devise. We must have some means of social reproduction, but it is arbitrary whether we choose monogamous marriage or the many other possibilities that exist. Cultures, groups of people, create preferred ways of doing these things, standards against which they judge performances by their own members and outsiders. Looking at the issue very generally, the major contentious question for many of our culturally loaded activities is whether some ways of performing them, some standards, can be shown to be objectively superior to others. What is not in doubt is that all human groups fabricate standards of some sort in the space left undetermined by the physical world.

In some sense, it is this anthropological use of culture which must provide the limits of our educational activities because if something does not exist within our culture then we cannot pass it on. However, this limiting notion does little more than this if we are considering educational choice. And its failure here derives from the obvious fact that in any reasonably developed culture—and by this we mean any culture that is minimally complex—there is both too much to consider passing on *in toto* and, and just as importantly, there are some things we cannot pass on to individual children, some things we do not want to pass on, and some things which we may wish to pass on but we do not think school is the best place for this to be done.

Let us deal with these limitations one by one. In a complex culture such as our own, tensions always exist between different points of view. There are people who, for instance, regard football or books or music or simply lying in the sun as the most important aspect of life and others who regard all or some of these things as a total waste of time. We cannot possibly hope or intend to pass on both of these attitudes to individual children. To do so would be incoherent. Therefore, with any of these items, we have to decide within education whether we touch upon the item at all and, if we do, what type of attitude we wish to encourage towards it.

Such selection is helped by the second point. If we look around our culture there are many things which we positively do not wish our children to inherit, 'cultural liabilities' in Martin's phrase (1999). The obvious candidates here are those things within our culture which we regard as immoral, for example financial dishonesty, cruelty and racism; but such things stretch beyond the immoral to the simply nasty—we may not think pornography immoral but, even so, we might not want our children exposed to it. So, if something is generally considered nasty this provides a defensible reason for not including it within our educational system.[1]

There are plenty of other things in our culture which are not nasty but which most people would see as having no place in education—the trivia and banality of everyday life. The trivial excludes itself because any education system with limited time and resources, and this includes all education systems, would be simply wasteful if it dealt in trivia. The banalities of life within a particular culture are, by their nature, likely to be passed on outside the education system and therefore, again, it would be a waste of time for that system to deal with such things. All education systems assume both that much is known already by the children and that much will be learned outside the actual institutions of education. Although care is needed here because some groups in our society may not grasp what, in general, we assume to be the banal stuff of everyday life, this shows the need for sensitivity on the part of those in education and, perhaps, some possibility of remedial education for such groups; it does not require a re-orientation of the education system as a whole.

As well as the nasty, the trivial and the banal we can also exclude the truly esoteric from our education system. It is probably the case that somewhere in our culture there are individuals fascinated by, and perhaps skilful at, tracking (say) but—and we are, of course, only thinking of *our* culture—such a skill is not one the generality of people would want passed on in our schools. This is an extreme example but it applies to more important things. Much of people's working lives is spent dealing with esoteric technicalities, such as the knowledge and skills one needs to be a widget maker, but such knowledge and skills, simply because of their limitations of scope, have no place within a general education system.

The exclusion of the nasty, trivial, banal and esoteric has pushed most theorists of education towards a second definition of culture. Culture in this sense is:

(2) The intellectual and artistic beliefs and practices of a given group of people or society.

The use of 'intellectual' and 'artistic' here is—at least for the moment—wide. So, for instance, in English culture the intellectual would cover things like chess as well as physics and the artistic would cover craft, such as furniture-making, as well as, say, music and painting. (Within a sub-group such as music this liberal interpretation lets in things such as punk rock as well as Elgar.) However, this narrowing does, at least at first blush, exclude things such as cricket and football (we shall look again at this in Chapter 4).

However, even this narrower idea of culture presents us with an impossibility as far as education is concerned. If we think of our culture existing historically as well as in the present—and a concern for history just is part of our culture—then it is, again, obvious that no limited education system can transmit all of that. We could, of course, simply choose to carve up our culture historically and plump for the transmission of only our contemporary culture or the culture of some slice of the past. The second of these suggestions, that we only teach about English culture in, say, the sixteenth century, seems both arbitrary and odd. The first shares certain problems with the second, but also has its own difficulties. One of the chief of these is that our past permeates our present. So, for instance, if we look at the biggest selling or most widely performed playwright in contemporary England, then we are likely to be looking at Shakespeare rather than any of our contemporaries. If we wish to teach Shakespeare properly, we have to teach something about the sixteenth century. But there is another objection, echoing what we said about culture in the anthropological sense, which is fatal to both these proposals. And that is that for any time slice, whether modern or ancient, the intellectual and artistic beliefs and practices, in our liberal sense of the word, will, at the very least, include much that is trivial, banal and esoteric. This is merely to say that much of the thought and art of any age is simply bad on its own terms. Whilst the study of poor examples may be pedagogically instructive and fascinating historically (it is both interesting and salutary to find, for instance, some nineteenth-century scientists being convinced that the key to human character is contained in the bumps on our heads) if we sincerely wish to pass on our concern for intellectual and artistic matters then indulgence has to stop here. What we need is not the second definition of culture but rather a third one of the kind Arnold championed. Culture in this sense is:

(3) The best intellectual and artistic beliefs and practices of a given group of people or society.

The notion that education should be thus concerned with the best is not, currently, a popular one. But before we go into some of the difficulties—and our answers to these difficulties—it is worthwhile pointing out some of the advantages of this approach to education. We do not, for instance, run into the problems of triviality and banality, which we mentioned above. If something is thought the best within the life of the intellect and arts, then it cannot be trivial or banal (and even processes that in some way make the rare familiar, for example the use of images from Monet for commercial packaging and cards, do not—or should not—undermine the quality of the real thing). But if the best cannot be trivial or banal, can it fall foul of some of the other filters we mentioned above? Can it, for instance, be nasty or esoteric? The answer for both of these categories seems to be a qualified yes. So, for example, although there has been debate as to whether it is possible to have pornographic art, such a possibility does, at first glance, seem to exist. And therefore if we exclude the pornographic from our education system we also have to exclude, at least at some levels, such art.

As far as the esoteric is concerned, there are areas of our intellectual and artistic lives which commend themselves only to the very few, for example sixteenth-century miniature painting or some of the intricacies of formal logic, and this fact alone might be reason enough for us to hesitate in beginning with such areas if our aim is to introduce our children to good painting in general or good logic in general. However, this is purely a procedural matter. We would not be concerned at all if an individual finished up being fascinated by such things, although they are hardly the stuff of introductory studies (and introductions may take years).

EDUCATION AND SCHOOLING

The main focus of our discussion lies on what schools and other parts of the formal educational system should be doing. It is important to recognise the range of other institutions and activities that perform educational functions, and it might be valuable, if quixotic, to aim at having them recognise their educational role, as Martin (1999) has recently urged.[2] Martin adumbrates a conception of cultural wealth that goes far beyond the high culture to which we mainly attend, and she notes that formal schooling preserves and transmits only a minuscule fraction of those riches. There is no doubt but that the stock of a culture, culture in the first two senses above, contains much of great value, as also some things it would be better without—our concern for high culture does not require us to say that *only* high culture is valuable; after all, the culture's stock contains everything the social formation does. But it would be utterly implausible to suppose that the formal school system should set itself to preserve and transmit all that. Marx may have imagined a society in which you are a hunter in the morning, a farmer in the afternoon and a sculptor in the evening, but even he must have recognised that no one could sensibly set out to master all the activities of any complex social group. In agreement with Barrow (1981), we see one of the main tasks of the formal school system as providing everyone with the intellectual tools that allow them to lead satisfying lives. It has to operate at a level of generality above the myriad particular occupations and roles that people may find themselves in. Since intellect imbues not only thought but feeling, not only reason but emotion and one's attitudes, formal schooling should set before people not only the best we have done with respect to understanding the world and our place in it but also the best we have done by way of living a life in it.

One of Martin's points is that education as the preserving and transmitting of cultural wealth is the business of many other institutions and that by in effect identifying education with schooling we can too easily forget and ignore the challenges confronting education in this wider sense. But here we come upon an important issue—the good is not necessarily to be conserved. Martin strikingly draws attention to the fact that while so much of our thinking is founded on a presumption of scarcity 'we forget that in the case of culture the issue is superabundance' (1999, p. 24). When the loss of a good results in less value overall it probably is right to attempt to conserve that good. But superabundance and culture's vitality mean that when one thing is lost others perhaps equally or even more valuable take its place. In the light of the enormous and irreversible changes human beings are making to the environment of their own and other species it is easy to miss the force of this point, but Martin's examples must give us pause: the know-how of tribal herbalists or old-time farmers might simply now be irrelevant just as the know-how of lamplighters has become irrelevant. Cultures change; old activities and ways of speaking die out and are replaced by others. It may be that the modern Western industrial or post-industrial world shows on balance a loss of valuable activities and their replacement by mindless labour, or unemployment, and pre-packaged entertainment; but the mere facts that some item of a culture's stock at one time is valuable and that it dies out are not enough to show that anyone had a duty to preserve it. We are not necessarily worse off for no longer speaking like Chaucer.

THE LOGIC OF 'THE BEST' AND THE AIMS OF EDUCATION

In constructing a curriculum, or indeed in many other contexts, appeal to the 'best' seems to have another benefit. If it is admitted, within any realm, that such a characterisation makes sense—and we will try to give it sense in Chapter 3—then exposure to this 'best' seems self-justifying. So, for instance, if we wish to introduce people to areas as diverse as football or wine tasting then taking them to watch Brazil play or getting them to taste Chateau Lafite seems obviously justified by the simple fact that these just are 'the best' in those areas (in a real sense they may be the best of the best). If you are invited to dinner and you ask, in an unmannerly way, why your host is giving you one wine rather than another, then to be told that it is the best—or the best they have—is sufficient answer. (Any response to this along the lines of 'I can't possibly appreciate it' or 'Chateau Plonk would have done' seems either like mock modesty or, even if true, does not disturb the force of the answer.)

So, once we have discerned the best in any particular field, this gives us reason to expose someone to it, if we wish to teach them about the field. It might be thought that asking people to choose the best that has been thought or done is then pretty straightforward. But it is not. We can see that by taking a simple example. Brian Lara currently holds the record for a batsman in a test match. His innings in Antigua is in that sense the best there has been. But if we wanted to point to the best innings any cricketer has played in a test match it might be that we would choose someone else's, thinking perhaps of the grace and power of the stroke-play or the strategic thinking revealed in its course or the difficulty overcome or some other feature. The basic point is that 'best' inherits the gappiness of 'good'; if something is a good X it is good in some respect or respects but not necessarily in all. Only in the rather unlikely event that something is not merely good but the best in all respects that we regard as relevant[3] would there be one unchallenged best X to be identified.

One way we could achieve this narrowing of the field would be if there were only one respect we did regard as relevant. But this is not going to help us in our case, since there are several purposes we want to pursue through educational activity and what is best for one may not be much good for another. It is a commonplace of educational thought that things are here very complicated indeed. If we consider science, for example, schools have different aims to pursue—we may want to convey what we currently believe to be the truth about something or we may want to give learners a grasp of a scientific way of thinking and investigating. The best answer as regards what we take to be true may not, for any number of reasons, display in an easily accessible way what we think of as quintessentially scientific procedures.

Again with respect to whatever we think is sufficiently good in either of these respects we have a tactical question of how to present it at a particular stage in a developing curriculum. What we tell an eleven-year-old of Mendel's experiments with peas will differ from what we teach at a higher school level and that will differ again from what we do in an advanced seminar on experimental methods and research ethics. In thinking about literature we might equally well consider it self-defeating to try to introduce *Othello* to eight year-olds. Having said this, it is worth remarking that much of the education that goes on in our schools does seem chronically to underestimate the capabilities of children and we therefore have to ensure that we have a realistic expectation of their capabilities before we decide what they can and cannot appreciate or understand.

The essential point remains that, in moving to practical conclusions, anyone endorsing the Arnoldian approach has still to consider exactly which ends are to be aimed at and how to bridge the gap between where learners are and what it is we want them to acquire.

ON IDENTIFYING CULTURES

To move to practical conclusions another set of issues must be addressed. We need to be able to specify which culture or cultures we are initiating people into and we have to be able to locate particular items within one or more such cultures. It is usually assumed that we can differentiate British—or English—culture from French or Chinese culture and identify what belongs in each. And, at various levels, it might be possible to do exactly this. So, for example, it may be the case that there is a particular Englishness to such things as Morris dancing, works for double string orchestras, and certain styles of landscape gardening. However, with other cultural items such a discrimination seems impossible or pointless. British science is not something that can usefully be marked off from science elsewhere, certainly not in an educational context. To be in the business of science, wherever one starts that business, is to be part of a worldwide community. Music and painting in England are not simply English music and painting, and an education which tried to teach people about such things whilst insisting upon national boundaries would be absurd in its parochialism. The English may be embarrassed that they gave the world cricket and football—because the world seems rather better at them than they now are—but once given, their efforts are then located on a world stage rather than on a purely national one. In consequence we see the educational system as having to embark on a kind of dialectical interaction, promoting its local culture but at the same time recognising the various wider traditions within which it exists, and, as we shall note in Chapter 6, the various other traditions some of its students may inhabit.

It may be difficult to allocate some cultural items exclusively to one cultural tradition. Are the writings of James and Conrad part of English literature or part of the literatures of America and Poland?[4] What do we say of a work such as *The Interpreters* by Wole Soyinka, which may have been produced in Nigeria but which uses a non-Nigerian form, the novel, and is written in a language, English, which many Nigerians cannot understand? Even extending the literature examples so that we talk about the novel in English, rather than the English novel, will not take us far enough. Although no one these days, we think, would share Arnold's confidence that the cultured Englishman would be able to approach Greek and Latin texts in the original language and read, say, Mann and Sartre in German and French, there would be something seriously awry with any initiation into English high culture which did not suggest that some knowledge of such texts and such writers—albeit in translation—did not constitute part of what it meant to be cultured in this sense of the word. Of course, geography and history play their part here. We expect acquaintance with the European masters but have no such expectation concerning knowledge of great writers or painters of Japan and China. Our culture, at every level, is suffused with influences from the European classical past—see how many fake Greek pillars you can count in a day surveying English domestic architecture—but we expect no such influence from Zen gardens. However, we have to exercise care even with those things which seem esoteric because distant. It is perfectly possible, for instance, to remain mostly in England and garner an expertise in Islamic carpets and Chinese landscape painting, and whilst it would be silly to demand that such an expertise is central to our cultural traditions it would be equally silly to overlook such possibilities.

OTHER FILTERS

The case for using the Arnoldian filter rests upon the apparently simple thought that one should prefer the better to the worse in a context where one cannot, or would not want to, have everything. But, as we have already said, this simple thought is far from popular. Before going on to flesh out this framework and deal with some of its difficulties, it is worth spending a little time on other filtering mechanisms which may seem more accessible than the search for the objective best.

Relevance

Relevance would seem to increase the utility of what is offered educationally, compared to something that is irrelevant. But the problem here is that relevance is not an intrinsic property but a relational one and one into which two other items have to be fitted. A piece of the curriculum—or the curriculum as such—has to be relevant both for someone, and for some particular purpose or goal. If we leave these slots unspecified, a little ingenuity is enough to show that anything is relevant for anybody. But an appeal to relevance itself cannot tell us how to start restricting what goes into these slots.

It is usually reasonably clear how to circumscribe the slot for the people involved. But even here there may be problems. Given some acceptable selection of goals, the number of items that are relevant for all members of the group, either at the time being considered or at any time in their subsequent existence, is likely to be pretty small. Relevance for all the group is then not going to provide enough. Relevance for some—but not others—seems *prime facie* unfair.

But it is the second slot, with regard to goals, which provides the real difficulties, and it is here that educators sometimes show their parochialism and lack of vision. So, for instance, it is sometimes thought obvious that home economics is more relevant for a young working-class girl than the study of Latin (see our discussion of Bantock on working-class education in Chapter 5). Well, she may be looking after younger siblings now but should we discount the possibility of a career in computing later (let us grant the classicists their claim to improve reasoning ability), or ignore the enhancement to her self-conception and view of the world which might come from acquaintance with Horace or Catullus? An appeal to relevance cannot decide whether to prefer enhancement of present activities to enhancement of skills which may be of use in the future; it cannot decide between economic or social or personal benefit. But these are some of the crucial issues for deciding upon a curriculum. Once such issues have been decided, once we have, for instance, decided that education should be the kind of enculturation which we envisage, then it may be that relevance can play a secondary role. Once, for example, we have decided that people should learn a second language, then it seems sensible to look around and see which one is spoken by their neighbours in the world—and for a large number of people in Britain this is more likely to be one of the languages from the Indian subcontinent than French—but even here relevance simply tells us what it might be sensible to offer the majority. It does not, and it cannot, rule out the study of, say Serbo-Croat or Cantonese, for those individuals who wish to engage in such study.

Familiarity

Often mistakenly connected to relevance is familiarity or, more tendentiously, parochialism. Given that one has to start somewhere in putting a curriculum together, then it might be thought that it is easier to start with items which our children are already familiar with to some extent. Such familiarity may pay motivational dividends in elementary education. But it is crucial to see that this, even if true, is about where we start and not about where we end up. Nothing about the initial pull of the familiar requires us to deny that the direction of curriculum movement should be Arnoldian. It is crucial to keep this in mind because not to do so is to fail to see one of the most important functions of education: its capacity for transforming lives.

Education extends the range of the possible for people, it widens their horizons, it empowers them perhaps in a way that nothing else can do. If this seems too high flown, it is worth remarking that economic considerations also pull against the familiar: why spend vast amounts of money on schooling or education which does not take people very far from what they know already or can pick up on the street or from television?

As far as the motivational 'fact' mentioned above is concerned, it is a pleasing and pertinent fact that many children seem more interested in the dinosaurs and giants that they will never meet than in the dogs they do meet and the neighbours who own them. (And whilst local history may be interesting, it is also a fact that much of any country is covered by places where nothing much of general significance has happened.) So it may be the case that using the familiar is counter-productive in that it lacks the magic of the new and thus tells against the type of valuable transformation education can achieve.

Fundamentalism

This notion is of much greater interest and difficulty than the other filters we have been looking at. The basic idea is that what we have to teach forms some sort of structure analogous to a building, some parts supporting others. The idea is then that we should select these key parts, rather than the more peripheral. When we look at our propositional knowledge of the world, it is certainly tempting to try to cast it in some such way, and to see the world itself as built up in layers: sub-atomic particles; atoms; molecules; cells and other coherent things; systems of such things; systems of systems; and so on, each with their ways of working. Fundamental notions will tend to be general, and applicable in many different contexts. That generality may be won at the cost of spiriting away much of the detail of the different contexts, so one may think of them as highly abstract rather than concrete (though this contrast does not seem to us one that we should strive strenuously to preserve).

In other contexts, such as the arts, the way we cash the metaphor may be different. One way points in the direction of paradigmatic exemplars, the key achievements in a particular genre. As with fundamental theory in the sciences, this interpretation is likely to push us in the Arnoldian direction, under another description. While that is so, and perhaps often a welcome fact, we would repeat a point made earlier. To the extent that there are good grounds for preferring some sequencing of curricular material to others, it might not be best to invoke what is fundamental or paradigmatic, at least at the start. It may be possible to see set theory as fundamental to mathematics, but that does not entail that one should start children off with sets. Shakespeare or Joyce may not be the best ways into literature.

The thought behind an appeal to fundamentals is often that one cannot understand one thing without a prior understanding of something else, the more fundamental item. How could we teach acceleration before we have taught velocity? How could you understand Joyce's *Ulysses* before you have read the *Odyssey*? There are some dependencies of this sort, but they are not as strong as many people suppose. Whatever the cognitive states that underlie what we think of as understanding, they are a matter of more or less, and they allow for considerable variety between people. When there are separate routes into a topic, separate that is from the routes into what we think of as a more fundamental topic, we can get at least some understanding of the less fundamental one independently and prior to the more fundamental.

Let us try to spell this out in terms of the examples offered. Since in Newtonian terms force is needed for acceleration but not for uniform velocity, we have a route into cases of acceleration via experienced forces and so could get people thinking about motion from those cases rather than from simple uniform velocity. It is true that we might not get very far in explaining the associated mathematics, as that is usually presented, but our point is merely that what is often regarded as a paradigmatic case of conceptual dependence with sequencing consequences for a curriculum does not have such strict consequences.

It may be evident how we would comment on the case of *Ulysses*. A great deal of that work is accessible without picking up the resonances of Homer's epic, and in any case the nature of the awareness of Homer necessary for an adequate grasp of Joyce's book is by no means clear: do you need to have read Homer in Greek, in what sort of translation, or is the schematism offered by a critic like Gilbert enough? The undisputed fact of cross-reference here leaves a great deal indeterminate in how we should go about presenting the later work.

There are other ideas in this area. Some insist on going back to basics because much of what most people in our culture would consider for a fully developed curriculum can only be approached by people who have mastered certain basic skills. The obvious examples here are literacy and numeracy, without a grasp of which the study of literature or science cannot begin. Such basic disciplines are, in fact, over-justified for they not only provide the foundations for further study but they also provide children with skills without which their adult lives will be both difficult and limited. (But it is worth bearing in mind that if this second justification were sufficient, education in these things could stop at the primary level.)

The structuring of our knowledge manifests itself in education in another way. When we come to the developed disciplines themselves, their relationships are reflected in the timing of what we teach; so, for example, we teach physics, chemistry and biology at school, but we tend not to teach biochemistry. This is partly because the chemistry of living organisms is extremely complex and difficult, but partly because it makes both intellectual and economic sense if students master some of the basics of biochemistry in purely chemical contexts since they are chemical principles. With the study of the arts similar notions apply: the study of paradigmatic figures or movements, for example Shakespeare, Jane Austen, the painters of the High Renaissance, is both worthwhile in itself and also provides a key to much subsequent writing and painting. It may be possible to do without such a key to study, say, the work of the Pre-Raphaelites bringing in such Art History as is necessary but this is both more difficult and more limiting than the other approach.

Curriculum theorists will be familiar with yet another use of the notion of what is fundamental. Hirst's 'Forms of Knowledge' thesis (Hirst, 1965) was an attempt to delineate the fundamental types of rational thinking and use this to inform the academic curriculum. Unfortunately, some of the so-called Forms of Knowledge were only dubiously so (see Gingell, 1985; Barrow, 1976) and the justification offered for the package seemed far from compelling (see White, 1973). Hirst, in his later work (1993), seemed to acknowledge the type of concern for cultural practices which we are elucidating in this book, but without spelling out his suggestions.

Inasmuch as artists, or indeed members of any literate or quasi-literate tradition, refer to earlier works in their tradition, there is something to be said for a historical sequencing of guided exposure to the tradition. But familiarity, relevance and other factors push us much closer to the present. The moral, which is really the simple point we have been making, is that in many areas of understanding we are thrown *in medias res* and have to make the best of it. Conceptual or other dependencies may help us organise our ideas on a comparatively micro-level but we should not over-emphasise their importance.

A word of warning before we move on to other matters. When we are talking about the paradigmatic figures in intellectual or artistic traditions it is often easy to forget that such traditions are 'living' or, at least, ever-changing things. And such changes include revaluations as to what counts as part of the tradition or not and, perhaps, what counts as a paradigm or not. So, for example, not long ago the theory of continental drift was espoused only by geological cranks; now it is a fundamental element in our understanding of geology. For some the work of Charlie Parker may hardly count as music; for others, it provides a significant and formidable achievement in modern music. Fashions change and so does our understanding of the world, and such changes are reflected in our canons of excellence. Schools tend to be rather behind the times with regard to these matters; but very often the battles over the canons come to be played out, as farce rather than tragedy, at that educational level.

INSTITUTIONS

We shall try—in the next chapter—to show the possibility of identifying the best. But before that we need to do a further ground-clearing exercise. Before deciding how to get the best in our intellectual and artistic traditions, we have to be able to identify these traditions and their components.

If we are trying to ascertain what something is, what kind it belongs to, we often have to look at what people make of it. In some cases there is little or no such problem: is this stuff glucose, or is that an *Anopheles* mosquito that is troubling me? Here we just look more carefully, carry out various tests, and we have an answer. But if we want to know whether some plant is a weed, or some bit of language is a lyric poem, we have to do more than simply inspect the object, we have to see how it fits into human life. We may say that things of this second sort have an institutional aspect. A plant is a plant, but it becomes a weed when it thwarts someone's interest in other plants. Institutional aspects typically reveal a relativity to human purposes, but their basis may be an objective matter: some plants may indeed choke out, or merely get in the way of, those that we are interested in. Given the great diversity of human interests, institutional aspects often vary with different contexts or different people: one man's weed may be another woman's favourite house plant. Our grasp of the world may also make a difference: we may discover that what were thought injurious weeds actually promote or protect the plants we are interested in.

For our purposes, the utility of an appeal to institutions is that we can use a socially given identification of a kind without having to deny that it may be based on possibly complex sets of other conditions but equally without ourselves having to delineate such conditions. It permits us to set out some of the crucial distinctions we employ without further qualification.

Speaking generally of any institutional kind, X, we may say that there are at least three pertinent contrasts that we employ:

(a) X as against Y, where there is no question of rivalry or competition between X and Y (as we contrast fishing and gardening, geomorphology and genetics, Ming vases and Ife bronzes);

(b) X as against pseudo-X, where the pseudo-X is conceived as a comparatively disreputable competitor of X (as Popper contrasted science and pseudo-science, or we contrast poems with computer-generated 'poems');

(c) Better X as against worse Y (as we contrast Einstein's gravitational theory with Newton's, or Mozart's oeuvre with Salieri's, or Socrates' way of teaching with that advocated by Dickens' Gradgrind in *Hard Times*).

We claim that an appeal to the social institution decides what to count as these Xs, Ys and pseudo-Xs. The third case is paradigmatically a case of evaluation, of a kind we shall look at more closely in the next chapter. But very similar evaluations arise in the second case too. And, in some contexts, one could also see the first case as bringing an evaluation in train, although it is apparently merely a matter of identification. If you wish to achieve the typical ends of fishing, it would be pretty silly to engage in typical gardening activities.

ENTITIES AND AUTHORITIES

To pick out weeds or poems we need to identify the relevant social context, the appropriate expert authorities. In the case of plants, it is not difficult to pick out the relevant people: it is those who farm or professionally tend gardens, whose expertise counts in such matters. This does not, of course, mean that you cannot lovingly cultivate bindweed as a house plant. However, it does mean that most of the time we are wise to defer to expert judgement in areas where objective claims can be made (for example, if you plant this in your garden it will choke out, or interfere with, the other plants you are interested in). As with other experts they can make mistakes and they may differ amongst themselves; but nevertheless at any one time there is likely to be a broad institutional consensus on weed-hood. (Some of the differences get ironed out in functional ways: if you make the wrong kind of mistake as a farmer or gardener you end up without farm or garden.) So if we wish to cultivate plants one of the things we need to do is to identify the people who hold, or the institutions which embody, authoritative opinions on such matters.

Plants may be simple, poetry and physics are less so. But again, we have the institutions to help. It is usually fairly easy to identify poets—they write poems and publish them—and it is very easy to identify Professors of Poetry. The same is true with physics. But the poetry case is complicated by the pretensions of those who can see no reason why the efforts of their eight-year-old should not be considered on a par with Keats. The physics case is complicated by the fact that things like astrology make claims which make it sound like a science. Questions of identity thus get mixed up with the second and third contrast we set out above.

With the poetry case, on one level at least, we can afford to be tolerant. At this point in the discussion, after all, we are not after the best but only the type, so it is possible simply to include the efforts of eight year-olds as poetry, even if we expect our authorities to be able to give reasons why Keats is better. Much aesthetic theorising recently, and for good reason, has been concerned with the limits of art: for example, should André's pile of bricks, Duchamp's urinal or Tracey Emin's bed be included? And whilst it is certainly not problem-free, we are happy with the theory that says they should if the Art World says they should (see Dickie, 1974, Davies, 1991). After all, no question of quality is yet involved. (However, if you are teaching about art it might be a serious mistake to begin with disputed cases.)

With physics, and cognitive studies generally, the stakes are higher and such tolerance is out of place. Here one has areas of intellectual life which make claims to truth and such claims rule out the type of indulgence extended to poetry. A crucial dimension of value in such activities relates to this question of truth so that evaluative questions of both the types we distinguished above become much more pressing. The institutional approach accepts the distinctions currently in force and enforced by the relevant communities; a good deal of philosophising can be seen as attempts to justify those distinctions.

The example of astrology

In saying the institution or social tradition tells us what is good or bad science and what is pseudo-science, we are not denying that there may be general principles underlying these distinctions, though we are allowing ourselves the luxury of not having to identify them.

It may be instructive to look a little closer at the case of astrology which was usefully discussed in a paper by Thagard (1978). Thagard shows that simplistic attempts to demarcate science from pseudo-science by an appeal to one key issue such as verification, testability or falsification fail. On the one hand, astrology can produce testable claims—indeed they have been tested statistically and a few have been supported— and on the other, no reputable scientific theory is conclusively falsifiable. Some critics have urged its origins in magic and beliefs in cosmic 'correspondences' against astrology, but they seem not to notice that chemistry has the same parentage, and in any case historical origin says nothing about present status. The same can be said for the motivations of believers in astrology: it might provide solace in an otherwise empty world. But people may have the most bizarre motives for believing quite ordinary truths.

A more substantial issue is the fact that astrology assumes the operation of principles quite beyond the ken of the rest of our (scientific) world-picture. But on its own, that hardly makes it un- or anti-scientific. As Thagard remarks, Wegener's theory of continental drift had no mechanism to appeal to and, while for a long time it was certainly laughed at, it has triumphantly asserted its place within rather than outside geological science. He also remarks that we are now assured on statistical grounds of a link between smoking and cancer while remaining ignorant of the biochemical processes responsible. Both Thagard's examples might be faulted, since the scientific beliefs in question do not require mechanisms or processes of a quite unknown type, though it is certainly not obvious how one would go about distinguishing when a new theoretical notion is of a new type and when it is merely a new example of an existing type.[5] And another geological example might strengthen Thagard's position—the nineteenth-century controversy between naturalists and physicists about the age of the earth needed the discovery of radioactivity for its resolution, and that would surely have been, by the standards of the relevant physics, a radically new idea.

A final criterion Thagard considers is the fact that astrologers face various serious unresolved problems, such as whether to take the precession of the equinoxes or the planets discovered since Ptolemy's time into account in their derivations. But again, our accepted scientific theories usually face problems. The mere fact that astrology faces some too cannot count decisively against it.

Having examined separately the objections raised against astrology, Thagard then offers us an account of its pseudo-scientific status that explicitly recognises not only these broadly logical issues but also historical and social factors. Key among these are that astrology, or speaking generally any pseudo-science, 'has been less progressive [he explains this as 'a matter of the success of the theory in adding to its set of facts explained and problems solved'] than alternative theories over a long period of time, and faces many unsolved problems; but the community of practitioners makes little effort to develop the theory towards solutions of the problems, shows no concern for attempts to evaluate the theory in relation to others, and is selective in considering confirmations and disconfirmations' (1978, p. 228).

So his case against astrology is that it is 'dramatically unprogressive' and has changed little since the time of Ptolemy's formulation, it faces outstanding problems, there are now alternative theories of personality and behaviour available, and the community of astrologers is in general uninterested in dealing with the problems or comparing their theory with the others.

A consequence he welcomes is that on this sort of account a theory may be scientific at one time (as astrology was for Ptolemy and Kepler) but become pseudo-scientific at another. It is even possible on Thagard's account that astrology could regain its scientific status.

One point we want to draw from Thagard's account is the recognition that while there may be general features distinguishing regular science from fads and fallacies these features may not be obvious to those involved. Many scientists would, and did, attack astrology by reference to one or two features of the sort whose salience Thagard has given us reason to doubt. There is obviously a tremendous social pressure from peers and the whole scientific establishment that underwrites boundaries such as those between science and pseudo-science, and these pressures are usually much more than simply rational. This is not to say, on the other hand, that the boundaries are merely a matter of social power. But in general we think it salutary that educational theorists recognise the choices involved in excluding pseudo-sciences and in enforcing other such boundaries.

Other disciplines

The appeal to the socially given works well with the natural sciences and mathematics. If you want to find out what is or is not mathematical, ask a mathematician. This works despite the survival of various ethnomathematical systems and the internal split between classical and intuitionist mathematics. The case becomes much more complicated with the human sciences. Here again there are claims to truth being made. If Freud is right then behaviourism is wrong. But here the warring camps often do not recognise their rivals as engaged in the same battle. We can exercise tolerance here or we can take sides by indicating, perhaps with philosophical argument in support, which of the rivals we are prepared to recognise as authoritative. The history of medicine and the type of disputes now raging concerning alternative medicine perhaps point towards a sceptical tolerance as the wisest stance.

Another truth-claiming area where there should be battles, but there are only minor skirmishes, is that of religion. Partly this is because of the present dominance of monotheistic faiths, although we, like Hume, can see no advantage to a one-god model over a many-god model as an explanatory hypothesis. Partly it is because such faiths can execute the Roman shuffle; your Artemis is my Diana, your Allah is my God. But partly, we suspect, it is because the wiser among theologians realise that to make trouble for any religion is to make trouble for all. So, for instance, if you make a fuss about the manifest unfairness of British blasphemy laws, where you can only blaspheme against Christianity, you are liable to end in a situation where the laws are fair to all because they simply cease to exist.

Along with this curious tolerance among what appear to be conflicting religions there is an almost total silence on the second of our contrasts above, that between 'genuine' religion and pseudo-religions. Whereas we can find philosophers of science reflecting on the justification for decrying astrology, we cannot so easily point to philosophers of religion who have attended to the distinction between religion and cults or superstitions (but see our discussion of Phillips in Chapter 5), though there has been some anthropologically inspired work on magic. When we attend to the educational context and the question of what to include in the curriculum, religion also confronts us with an issue not raised by any other intellectual activity in the curriculum—the wholesale denial of its object, in other words, atheism.

So far we have tried to sketch out what is intended by an institutional account of cultural activities. Briefly, art is what the art world says it is. Science is what scientists, and some others, say it is. This means that in order to identify activities and their products we have to identify either—in most cases—the group of people involved in such activities or—in some cases—a smaller group among a larger group of claimants whose judgement we trust. This institutional account, we stress, is primarily a method of deciding whether something is of a certain type or not and this is a different question from whether a particular item within the type is a good example of the type or not. Sometimes one way of dismissing what someone takes to be an egregiously bad item of type X is to deny its Xhood. So to some, *The Rite of Spring* or Jamaican Dub are not even music. Usually it is clear that this type of move is an exaggeration for rhetorical effect. These things are clearly pieces of music in the institutional sense. The interesting question is whether they have any musical value, and often those that use the 'not really X' move are doing so to protect their own criteria of musical value from scrutiny. (This way of using language is similar to a pervasive feature of evaluative language which can also lead to some problems—the use of, say, 'moral' either to characterise a whole range including the morally good and the morally bad or to indicate restriction to the good or acceptable portion of that range.)

Identifying better or worse

Identifying an X is different from judging that one X is better than another in certain respects. But whilst we have two questions here, the institutions usually provide both answers. It is normal for human activities to be graded as more or less competent, skilful, good or bad of their kind and the criteria for these sorts of judgements will be part and parcel of what the institutions' users embody in their thought and actions. It is unlikely, however, that over the matter of value all the members of the institution in question will speak with one voice. Therefore again we may be forced to choose between competing claims. The point here is that we want such choice, as far as it is possible, to be a rational one and this involves not only demanding that the relevant criteria be open for inspection, but also ensuring that we have reasons for going for this way of deciding rather than that.

The appeal to institutions gives us at least the accepted terms of evaluative debate, the issues that count, the distinctions that ought to be heeded. In both science and art, at the frontiers at least, there will be dissensus, and it is not immediately resolvable by reference to whatever makes decisions rational elsewhere within the field. If it were, these activities would be much easier than they are. There is an inescapable element of judgement in applying accepted criteria to contentious cases, but this fact does not of itself undermine the appropriateness of these criteria in other less contentious contexts.

Comparison between traditions

In distinguishing science from pseudo-science we are ruling out consideration of one way of doing things. But do we always have to do this? Appeal to the authoritative people will provide us with paradigmatic Thai opera or Thai curry. Appeal to another, but perhaps overlapping, set of people will do the same for a Monteverdi opera and pasta sauces. But suppose that we wish to judge between the two, curry or Bolognese? The criteria internal to traditions of music-making or cooking do not address this type of comparison across traditions.

But do we need to do this at all? Cannot we just, with either opera or food, go Thai today, Italian tomorrow? We have enormous sympathy with this approach in those cases where there seems to be no question of fit with the external world. However, here as elsewhere, time is short and practically some choices will have to be made, and it would be preferable if such choices were not the result of the toss of a coin. Also, the Arnoldian filter which tells us to go for the *best* that has been thought or done seems to presume some sort of judgement across traditions.

When such comparisons are within the same overarching cultural tradition, that tradition usually provides us with at least some ranking among its component activities. So Thai opera ranks higher than Thai village dances, *haute cuisine* ranks higher than bubble and squeak. But often these prestige rankings are based on grounds extrinsic to the activities themselves, whereas rational evaluation seeks to find something intrinsic to the activities that can be used to discriminate.

Cross-activity comparisons involve the pretension that we can somehow stand outside particular activities to find a basis upon which to judge between them. Looking at the problem abstractly (we shall return to it in more concrete forms in subsequent chapters) it would seem that one might make progress by working from the bottom up, by starting with the criteria given by traditions for the particular activities, looking at closely related activities and their criteria and trying to discover the shared traits. The process can be continued, working to encompass an ever-wider range until no further useful progress can be made. At that point one might claim to have reached an enumeration of the key kinds of activity it is worth distinguishing.

Of course in practice things are not going to work out as neatly as this story supposes. One of the most important qualifications is that in reality the criteria we uncover are not all nicely compatible with each other. We are familiar with very broad distinctions such as classical versus romantic, or a taste for elaborate complexity as against elegant simplicity (Escoffier versus Guérard), where the contrasting groups can seem to define away the opponent's value, rather than merely define it differently. But in general we can expect different criteria to pull in often opposing directions: clarity against evocativeness, simplicity or unity against verisimilitude.

Related perhaps to these internal tensions is the fact that we recognise different styles of doing what, at a more general level, we can regard as pretty much the same thing. We typically do distinguish between the approach to tragedy embodied by, say, French classical drama and that of Shakespeare or of the Greeks. Within those stylistic traditions it may be useful to discriminate, but while we can learn from comparisons between the different schools should we really aim to place *Phèdre* above or below *King Lear* or *Antigone*? Yet with these styles, at least, we are back with one of the crucial levels of cross-activity comparisons we are dealing with.

However, just as we earlier supposed that the process of comparing similars and drawing out shared criteria of excellence could go on until it ran out of steam, thereby yielding the fundamental categories of activity worth distinguishing, so we can suppose a related process of identifying styles, schools, traditions which it is better to recognise than to obliterate in the march towards the most general standards. In neither case should we expect to reach a final unchanging consensus, even on past activity. But we can hope that sympathetic appreciation of the variety of human achievement will provide more than enough categories of excellence to be going on with in the educational enterprise. And the aim, in that enterprise, should not be the rigid transmission of dogma but a grasp of what is essential for the continuing life of the mind.

The limits of high culture

After these general remarks about institutions let us focus a little more on what things fall within the artistic and intellectual practices of the traditions we are concerned with. It might be thought that the answer is given by our second definition of culture as the intellectual and artistic beliefs and practices of a given group of people or society. And, indeed, in crude terms it is. Given a list of items which included, say, writing poems, painting, bed making, walking, doing physics, making films and drinking beer, most people would have little hesitation in placing items one, two, five and six (poems, paintings, physics and films) within the ambit of the definition and the others without. The central examples of high culture are not in doubt, though we wish to insist that most writers with an interest in education have tended not to notice the non-literary components such as music, dance and painting. But simply because it is clear that some boundary exists here, this does not mean that the exact nature of that boundary is clear. On what side of this boundary is photography? Or car maintenance? Or widget making? Or butterfly collecting? To answer such questions needs a rather fuller account than that already given. We suspect that, as Wittgenstein remarked of the line between the umbra and penumbra, in the end the line here will have to be drawn rather than discerned, and it may be drawn with a broad brush rather than a fine pencil. However, some clues might be found to indicate the general area for the final line.

One suggestion made, for instance, by Bantock (1967) is that we can roughly delimit high culture by looking at the type of activities on offer at our universities and institutions of higher education. These, so to speak, are the line drawers for our society. There is merit in this suggestion but its use needs caution. Partly this is because we may still want to sift out of the cultural scene—in this sense of the word— some of the things taught in such institutions. So, for instance, engineering, business studies and dentistry are all well established at the level of higher education but we can imagine objections to these being included within a list of high cultural activities. Partly it is because the role of higher education has been subjected to serious criticism in recent years. According to writers such as Bloom (1987) and MacIntyre (1990) higher education is in crisis because of internal fragmentation and external pressure. Whereas such institutions once had a clear idea of their place and function within our culture, this clarity of vision and purpose has now been lost. There is a certain apocalyptic feel about the comments of both writers. Both seem to subscribe to a notion of a golden age when all was well—although it is telling that for Bloom this is pre-1968 and for MacIntyre it seems to have been found in the Scotland of the eighteenth-century Enlightenment—and both seem to seriously exaggerate the divisions within higher education. It is certainly true that, within universities, philosophers may not understand the doings of sociologists and art historians may be baffled at the work of theoretical physicists, but in all probability this is to do with the increasing specialisation of the particular academic disciplines, rather than the advent of a postmodern Tower of Babel.

There have been other reactions to this supposed crisis. Barnett (1988), for example, thinks we have reached a position where 'truth', 'objective knowledge' and 'rationality' can no longer be understood in their traditional senses and therefore cannot be pursued by university teachers and students in such senses. Instead, he thinks, following Habermas' critical approach to knowledge, we need to reveal to students that 'all is ideology'. By dedicating higher education to reflective teaching and learning and emphasising student freedom, we can then aim at the emancipation of the student body.

Unfortunately for Barnett, the first part of his claim is simply false and his solution is self-defeating. A quick glance at something like Dancy and Sosa's *Companion to Epistemology* (1992) shows that 'truth', 'objective knowledge' and 'rationality' are still very much alive in their traditional senses and continue to be the focus of the vast majority of work within epistemology. As to the notion that 'all is ideology', this, if true, applies to the notion itself, that is, if *all* ideas are ideological then *this* idea *must* be; but this means that Barnett's aim of 'emancipation' comes down to little more than replacing one ideology with another.

It is probably true that our universities are less clear about their role in our culture than they were a hundred years ago. It is not true that the past was a time, within such institutions, of sweetness and light and of noble application to a common purpose. Even a cursory glance at the medieval universities reveals places riven by violent— often physically so—dispute. And whilst modern academic departments may wonder at the work of other departments, the last burning of books in a university in England took place in Oxford in 1684. But if we can, as we think, ignore the cries of doom that arise from some quarters concerning our institutions of higher education, this does nothing for our original problem. Given such institutions, and what goes on in them, how do we decide what is high culture and what is not?

It will help here, we think, to attend for a moment to what seems a rather different task of demarcation. Collingwood, in his *Principles of*

Art (1965), seeks to distinguish art from craft. Whilst his attempt fails in his own terms, because of failures within his own general theory, it can, if understood as an attempt to distinguish intrinsic and extrinsic value, help us in our present task.

1   Craft involves a distinction between means and ends.
2   In crafts there is a distinction between planning and execution. A craftsman always knows what he wants to produce before he produces it and such knowledge is always precise—not a table of indeterminate size but a table six feet by three.
3   Means and end are related in one way in the process of planning—the thought of the end precedes the means, and in the opposite way in execution—here means are prior to end.
4   There is a distinction between raw material and finished product in the crafts.
5   There is a similar distinction between form and matter. In crafts the craftsman gives a different form to matter.
6   The crafts are either hierarchically related to one another, in that one supplies the matter for another, or hierarchically organised within themselves.

The arts, Collingwood argues, are not like this. First, there is no real distinction between means and end when, for instance, a poet is composing a poem in his head. Second, although in some arts there may be a distinction between planning and execution, for example when an architect builds a building, in others the work may come into being without planning. Third, because means and ends, and planning and execution cannot really be distinguished in some arts, then there cannot be an ordered relationship between the items of each pair. Fourth, to believe that a playwright uses raw materials in the same way that a blacksmith does is simply to confuse two very different processes. Fifth, if we can give no real sense to the notion of raw material in the arts, we can also give no sense to the notion of the artist imposing form upon this raw material. Lastly, there is nothing in the arts which really resembles the hierarchies we find in the crafts.

It is difficult, in a general sense, to understand what Collingwood thinks he is doing here. It is certainly the case, as he points out, that the production of some works of art does not exemplify the characteristics he takes to typify the crafts. However, it is equally true that many works of art do exhibit craft processes. Thus architects, potters, sculptors and painters—categories Collingwood recognises as artists—do make distinctions between means and ends, may often plan, and in their plans pay attention to raw material. In the work of the first three, at least, we can see a distinction between form and matter and we can, in some arts, for example architecture or more contentiously film-making, discern the type of hierarchy that Collingwood thinks only exists within the crafts.

It may be that he was merely trying to correct what he took to be an overly technicist view of art. And this his examples succeed in doing. But the force and extent of his argument seems to promise more than this. So, for instance, in his extended treatment of portraiture (1965, Ch. III) he wants to insist that the portrait painter who merely seeks for a likeness must be a mere craftsman. Real artists, although they *may* use craft techniques within their work, always transcend such techniques.

We suspect that the points Collingwood makes concerning the art/ craft distinction are better understood in terms of the final outline of his overall theory. Here, notoriously, he holds that because art is the product of the imagination works of art are imaginary objects whose primary existence is in the mind of the artist. Given such a conception, it is little wonder that he wishes to belittle any craft-like elements which appear to exist within the arts. But this final position is notoriously fraught with difficulties. It seems to divorce both the imagination and the terms we use to refer to artists—painter, poet, novelist—from any public criteria we might have for using those labels and, in doing so, makes otiose our actual use of such terms. It may be the case that there are fine, imaginative poets who keep their poetry locked in their own heads but such examples cannot possibly be the paradigm case of our use of 'fine', 'imaginative' or 'poet'. Such cases only make sense in a secondary way which depends upon a primary use which ties these concepts to public performances. And if this is true of poets, because of the public nature of language, it is doubly true of some of the other arts. The suggestion, for instance, that one could be a painter or an architect without actually painting or producing a design for a building seems simply incoherent.

It is for these reasons that Collingwood's theory receives little support today. Nevertheless, it may be the case that we can rescue some of his points without endorsing his untenable view of art. So, for instance, if we take the widespread notion of the arts which associates them with the production of things of intrinsic value, that is, things which are not valuable as a means to other ends but valuable in and for themselves, then many of Collingwood's points seem to make sense. The would-be artist who seeks to subordinate his or her art to anything else, for instance to moral message or the pleasure of patrons, runs the risk of losing the status of artist and becoming instead a propagandist or mere hack. But even here we must be careful. Great architecture must go beyond function but it cannot leave function behind. The builder of a church in which one cannot worship or a university in which one cannot study has not made a technical but forgivable mistake, but rather undermined his or her whole status as architect. But, this said, we can give some general sense to Collingwood's thoughts on art and craft via this notion of intrinsic and extrinsic ends. Thus, if someone makes something to serve some end beyond the thing made, whether this something is a portrait or pot, then to that extent they are acting as a craftsman. Even if they conceive of what they are doing in terms of intrinsic ends, for instance they simply want to make the perfect washer, if such an end can only be understood as a means to other ends, then they are engaged in craft whether they fully realise this or not. And such crafts are, as Collingwood points out, typically hierarchical. However, if the activity in question is aimed at the production of something that may be good in and for itself, then we have crossed the boundary from craft to art. Nor does it matter in such a case whether a part of the value still lies in some function the object serves or may serve. One may, for instance, use a beautiful vase to hold flowers or a beautiful building to pray, but in both cases the beauty cannot merely reside in the function served. One of the things we have here is a distinction within crafts as normally understood. There are crafts on this account which, at least in some of their aspects, cross over into the arts—let us call them art/crafts—and they do so because they are concerned with producing works of intrinsic value, such as a beautiful vase or table, rather than producing things which simply serve an extrinsic end. If a craft simply does the latter— let us call such things craft/crafts—then their value must be subordinate to that of the end they serve and therefore they in themselves cannot be seen as one of the ends of culture (care is needed here because, for instance, the photographer's craft may constantly cross these boundaries so that a photograph which was intended as journalism becomes something valuable in itself).

We can extend Collingwood's points, as we have glossed them, and add them to the points we made concerning higher education above. We may then go some way to drawing the line around the practices of high culture. In any culture there will be objects and activities which are valued in and for themselves. They may also serve other functions but their value is not subsumed by such functions and they may, like an elegant and graceful bridge which cannot bear the weight of modern traffic, continue to be valued even if their functional role has disappeared. Such things and activities will, typically, be the objects of celebration within the culture concerned. Such celebration may take the form of education so that the realisation of the worth of such things can be passed from generation to generation. However, it is unlikely that education will simply be concerned with such things. People must eat and live in a modicum of comfort before they can engage in such celebrations of intrinsic value and much of education, at all levels, will concern itself with these basic goals. But it is only in going beyond these basics that we begin to give flesh to the notion of high culture within a worthwhile life. Such celebrations will again typically go beyond the scope of education and there will be places such as museums and art galleries, and times in concert halls and playhouses, set aside for the display of the things in question, not so that we may learn from them, although this may happen, but simply so that we may enjoy them. The limits of high culture, in this sense, are the limits of these activities which show us to be the creators of these types of value. But even given this double set of criteria, content of higher education plus end-in-itself, we may not solve all our problems. What, for instance, do we do with the butterfly collecting mentioned earlier? As zoological enquiry it is obviously subsumed under science, but what if its aim is simply an aesthetically satisfying display? Here and elsewhere we suspect the activity in question inhabits the no-man's-land which any broad demarcation line will create. But enough has been said to serve our original purpose.

COGNITION AS PART OF ARNOLDIAN CULTURE

We have tried to draw a fairly traditional line between art and craft. What should we say about our cognitive activities? We endorse Gellner's perspective on the modern world:

> just as the notion of civil society is hardly usable unless the state is neatly defined and circumscribed and delimited, so the notion of culture does not really make much sense until strictly referential, growth-oriented knowledge has hived off under the name of 'science'. (1989, p. 206)

Using 'culture' in Arnold's way, we want to continue to include science *within* it, but we do not deny the points Gellner was much concerned to stress with respect to the singularity and unprecedented nature of science in the modern world. As he remarked in one of his last works:

> A world doomed to starvation, inequality, oppression and superstition, and one in which...there is not much knowledge over and above 'intimations' contained in 'traditions' is totally different from a world in which affluence and liberty are at least possible, and within which there is genuine knowledge, independent of any one tradition and transcending them all. (Gellner, 1996, p. 633)

Serious knowledge is now scientific or at least aspires to the condition of science. Scientific knowledge is transforming not merely our cognitive perspective on the world but the world itself that we inhabit. Technology once ran almost independently of theoretically charged scientific experimentation and speculation; now it does not. It is for these reasons that we think it essential that anyone educated in the modern world should be given adequate insight into both what the sciences have revealed and how they operate.

Arnold noted that science's account of things came without emotional colouring, but it is arguable that he somewhat under-estimated both the extent of the transformation it forces upon more traditional world views, particularly when turned upon our own valuing and our other purposes, and the extent that it embodies and inculcates certain values itself (disinterestedness, various cognitive virtues).

Their centrality to modern life put science and mathematics—in general terms—at the heart of any education into high culture for our times. It is probable that other important aims of responsible schooling will find it necessary to tackle many specific aspects of science and technology: to the extent that we want schooling to give people an informed grasp of the world they are living in it is necessary for such schooling to provide students with some level of under-standing of contemporary electronics, telecommunications, biotech-nology and ecology.

Given the vast range of the sciences we might teach, it is useful to consider whether we can find principles to select among them when our concern is with cultural and not more mundane matters. One answer would be to focus on those parts of science that address, and perhaps in some cases finally answer, questions of the kind Arnold invokes by speaking of what most concerns mankind, questions in other words of traditional moral and philosophical import. We stress the breadth of literature, music and the plastic arts, but we have not sought to deny that many of the supreme works in these modes address the 'big issues': what in overall general terms is the world like, what is the place of the human species in the universe, what sort of life should we lead? Philosophy, in Greece and elsewhere, began as a way of addressing these sorts of question and differentiated itself from the arts by a reliance on discursive reasoning rather than imaginative portrayal. (This differentiation, particularly that between philosophy and literature, is of course now increasingly called into question.) While in Greece it quickly developed obscure sub-disciplines and techniques, it kept returning to these sorts of synoptic questions, and its perspectives on them have become a central element in the educated thought of our tradition.

It is commonplace to see the development of science in the West as a progressive splintering of the encyclopaedic concerns of Aristotle into disciplines that can stand upon their own feet, leaving the unanswerable questions to an ever-withering philosophy. Serviceable though crude, such a picture should not encourage us to think that once a science has got started it no longer has anything to contribute to the philosophic enterprise. While no one would expect a philosopher to tell him anything about cosmology, we do continue to feel concerned by our place in the cosmos—Pascal's fear of the empty vastness of space remains pertinent, though we are not suggesting that any particular valuation of the human world can be derived from the cosmological facts—and it is to cosmologists we must now turn to let us know our best guess as to the nature of space and the universe.

An obvious, and we think vitally important, overlap between science and philosophy concerns those aspects of science that impinge on the reasonableness of traditional religious belief. Dawkins (1990) and Dennett (1996) have recently urged the decisive contribution Darwinian argument makes to overthrowing a theistic argument from design. No doubt their position can be challenged, but the point is simply that one is in no position now to reflect on the significance of marks of design unless one takes account of Darwinian argument. It is evident too that no responsible reflection on the distinctiveness of human nature can be undertaken in ignorance of Darwinian thought.

Cosmology and Darwinian evolution can then be seen as part of high culture because they address issues of crucial concern to other parts of that culture. But we can also make a case for the essential role of scientific reasoning as a cultural technique, the possession of which, if Gellner was right, has made the major difference between our social world and all others. Here we think it important to note that typically scientific information is treated in schools as dogmatically as any other. People learn to repeat what they have been told, but it is not alive for them, any more than the dates of significant historical events are things that they can personally relate to. To illustrate what we mean, consider what you would need to do to convince yourself on the basis of unaided visual observation that the earth is roughly spherical, that the moon reflects light from the sun, and so on—the astronomical facts that were known to the ancient Greeks. Or again, what grounds do you have for believing that table salt is NaCl or more generally that substances are made up of regular combinations of a restricted number of elements? We all know these things, but, we suggest, for most of us they are no better grounded than the wildest fantasy of religion.

We suggest then that a key component of our high culture is the amalgam of perspectives and techniques that people have labelled 'the scientific method'. We should expose students to its operations, and a comparatively easy way in is supplied by the sorts of issue we have just mentioned: the astronomy of the solar system and chemical atomism. These fields lead directly to the most fruitful and deepest of our physical theories[6] and they also show scientific reasoning at its particularly significant task of undermining and explaining away those beliefs we are encouraged to form on the basis of unschooled observation (see Brandon, 1989, for more extended discussion of science subverting common sense).

Mathematics belongs to high culture for similar reasons. It has been a paradigmatic example of pure reasoning at least since the Greeks reconstructed geometrical knowledge in an axiomatic system. It also makes a case for being seen as part of high culture as a necessary adjunct of any prolonged exposure to the physical sciences, but from the philosophical angle it has a place when it reveals something profound about the structuring of the world or something about the power of the forms of reasoning appropriate to it.

The human sciences have a claim upon our attention in the present context for the same reasons. To the extent that psychology or sociology or the other human sciences do tell us something we need to know, as humans trying to understand our predicament, then they deserve a hearing. As with mathematics and the natural sciences there are plenty of other reasons for giving them a place in schooling.

Of particular importance among these studies, we think, because it focuses on fundamentally important aspects of the human condition is what once flourished under the name of political economy. Not surprisingly economics has become riven between partisan supporters of radically different political persuasions, to the extent that it is difficult not to assume hidden commitments in those cases where political preferences are not already boldly displayed. But for people whose lives tend more and more to be removed from the exigencies of the production and distribution of food and other resources it is salutary to be reminded of our materiality, the scarcity of most of the goods we require or desire, and the workings of the various systems we have cobbled together to address these problems. In work such as Dasgupta's treatise on 'well-being and destitution' (1993) we can find a confluence of philosophical anthropology and fundamental economics of a kind that ought to contribute to responsible thinking about the future of humanity.

Of course, it is not only disciplines that aspire to scientific form that reveal much that is central to our self-conceptions. One of the central elements in high culture has been history. Here one might wish to make a distinction that applies with even more force in considering how to teach the sciences: one might aim to convey our current best view of the subject matter or one might aim to illustrate the sorts of understanding of human life and potentialities that we have achieved. A great historian becomes an element in high culture in his or her own right, and not only as a recorder of what has happened. We may subsequently correct the history but fail to deepen the insight as an understanding of the human condition.

It will come as no surprise, given what we have said on behalf of science, that some philosophy is also entitled to a place in an Arnoldian curriculum. We need not now enter into technicalities about when it would be appropriate—Plato notoriously recommended leaving it till past middle age, while in our own time Lipman would have it from the beginning of formal schooling. We are more inclined to agree with Lipman, and to consider that students can benefit not only from the tradition's reflections on the big issues but also from explicit study of defensible forms of reasoning (deductive, statistical and explanatory). The various other school subjects that claim to improve reasoning seem not to have much impact; it may be better to go straight to the teaching of reasoning (cf. Brandon and Sirbratthie, 1996).

NOTES

1. At least not on its own terms. We will expect learners eventually to be in a position to consider the case for and against pornography.
2. Martin argues that 'what is not considered an educational agent cannot in good logic be held responsible for its miseducative acts' (1999, p. 30). Not perhaps under that label, but if we have reason to think that a television advertising campaign, say, is increasing the number of violent crimes we can hold the advertisers responsible for that, and if it is encouraging people to think they need not worry about the validity of their deductive arguments we can blame it for that too. We should not call it miseducation when the agent sees itself merely as making money or entertaining people, but once it is an agent it can be held responsible for the effects of its actions or inactions. In thus criticising Martin, we are not suggesting that it would not be better to have the media, for instance, constrained by a public demand that they have and discharge educational responsibilities.
3. The restriction on what we regard as relevant is necessary since without it there would surely be no possibility of being best, or simply good, in every respect. If X is good with respect to A it is not usually going to be good with respect to the opposite of A. A painkiller is not likely to be good at inflicting pain.
4. The fact that Conrad wrote in English does not settle the matter. Ireland would claim Beckett for its own even though he wrote in French.
5. This difficulty is related to that discussed at the end of Chapter 1 of drawing a relevant and objective line between welcome new ideas and crazy ones.
6. Cf. Feynman's remark at the beginning of his lectures on Physics:

> if, in some cataclysm, all of scientific knowledge were to be destroyed, and only one sentence passed on to the next generations of creatures, what statement would contain the most information in the fewest words? I believe it is the atomic hypothesis... that *all things are made of atoms—little particles that move around in perpetual motion attracting each other when they are a little distance apart, but repelling upon being squeezed into one another* (Feynman, Leighton and Sands, 1963, pp. 1–2).

3

How to Choose the Best

This chapter deals with a crucial component of our position, the presumption that there are objective grounds for preferring one thing to another within the various cultural institutions we deal with, that there are better or worse symphonies, soufflés and theories of the atom. The task of showing this is more urgent for some institutions than others. While philosophers can doubt anything, most people are persuaded of the objectivity of our efforts to comprehend the physical world and to weigh, count and measure accurately in many areas of human activity. Again, when we are faced with a choice among functional objects or processes, most people will admit that we can ground a preference for a knife or an exercise routine on objectively established facts: sharpness, or measurable increase in strength. Here, certainly, various conflicting desiderata may enter and make actual decisions more difficult—the sharpest knife may also be the most expensive; we may need to worry about its safety features; it may be ugly; and so on. But many will doubt that our judgements of comparative worth for non-functional objects such as paintings or sonatas can claim a similarly objective basis. We shall, therefore, concentrate our efforts on the most doubted areas, but will begin with the less contentious, where we think it is useful to draw attention to the genuine problems some philosophers have stressed, to show in fact that what we believe to be popular unconcern deserves to be somewhat ruffled.

HOW TO CHOOSE THE BEST SCIENCE

We cannot here offer a comprehensive philosophy of science; indeed as with the philosophy of any other area there is no such settled thing to be had. Philosophy has its intractable problems, but they do not obstruct our getting on with things in the rest of the real world. What they can do is bring home to us that we have not yet achieved a final definitive picture, that we remain in a Socratic state of knowing that we do not fully know. The danger is, perhaps, of falling into a facile rejection of what we have actually learned.

We agree with the popular conception that science aims at truth. But in judging between scientific rivals, it is not simple truth that can

49

guide us. As the Popperians have insisted, with our scientific theories at least we cannot ever know that we know. Scientific theorising cannot be proved true by observational experiments, even when the results are in accordance with what the theories predict. As we noted earlier, we are on firmer ground in rejecting theoretical claims when the observational evidence goes against them, but even here there are complications (there are many introductions to the philosophy of science, among which we might single out Brandon, 1987). We may have nothing to indicate that anything is wrong with our theories but even that unheard-of situation would not be enough to establish that we have actually got it finally right. And of course mostly we do know that something is wrong (or at least incomplete) but we cannot yet correct it or fill the gap. For most of this century we have made do with fundamental physical theories, quantum mechanics and general relativity, that do not fit together. At the end of the nineteenth century, physics gave one answer for the age of the earth while geology gave a radically incompatible one, but there would have been no point in giving up on either discipline because their conjunction was inconsistent.

We might shift from simple truth to the signs we take as giving us some confidence in a theory's being better (closer to the truth, however that is to be construed, or whatever else may be taken as superiority here) than its rivals, but for the purposes of giving science its rightful place in high culture and implementing a feasible curriculum, that would not necessarily be the most instructive proceeding. Theories are idealisations cut to the essential points, without requiring all the qualifications messy reality requires—we enquire deeper if we think that everything falls with a constant acceleration towards the centre of the earth than if we attend to the fact that lead weights drop faster than feathers. The conventional history of Gallileo's work on inclined planes and Kepler's on the planets allows us to see the unification wrought by Newton more clearly than we would by starting with Einstein's corresponding derivations. In general, later work is often more difficult to comprehend, so it is convenient to go to the initial break-throughs rather than current understandings of the complexities. Still, one has to admit that there is a serious danger of fairy-tale 'history' here. It is tremendously difficult to get the history of science right. A 'Whig' history of science, in which progress is seen as the result of the decontextualised efforts of the 'great' scientific thinkers is extremely tempting. But it buys clarity, and perhaps excitement, at the expense of the manifest complexities of this field of human endeavour. To see science as a steady, upward series of marches from the ancients to the present day is to promote a view of the subject which simply ignores the radical discontinuities between then and now.

In science, as in the arts, there is a developing consensus on what work is exemplary and what is flawed. As in the arts the rush to immediate judgement can be embarrassing as is shown by prominent endorsement of Uri Geller's spoon-bending by a hitherto unknown force or the more recent furore over 'cold fusion'. Philosophers have liked to see these judgements of good and bad science as reflecting a concern for certain cognitive virtues. Our criteria for choosing among scientific theories make use of these notions; we suggest that more attention in education needs to be given to them rather than concentrating all attention on the content of particular, and often passing, theories.

Perhaps the first of these cognitive virtues that comes to mind is explanatory power, which is often associated with predictability. So falling apples and the moon's orbit are accounted for by appeal to Newton's force of gravity; the same force permits predictions of tides or the trajectory of ballistic missiles. Related to these notions is the idea of a theory unifying previously separate phenomena, or uncovering a mathematically expressible order in them. The developments culminating in Newton's work unified the physics of the heavenly bodies with terrestrial physics, and permitted the derivation of many apparently independent numerical relationships from a small number of fundamental laws. Of course not every mathematically expressible order is significant—Bode's 'law' that correlates planets' distance from the sun is now thought to register nothing particularly significant. Our present theories tell us, as far as they can, what is related and what is a mere coincidence.

Science is not just theory. Exemplary scientific work includes experimental ingenuity and care for the design of experimentation. These are among the craft elements of scientific technique. As in other areas there are difficult educational choices to be made as to how far people need to go in practising such crafts, but we suggest that at least they should be able to grasp the point of decisions here.

It is educationally valuable not to restrict our attention to the profound theories that address culturally significant issues. Students need also to consider quotidian science of the sort that is invoked to decide issues of public importance. Here attention to failings and errors is perhaps as useful as concentration on the exemplary, since there is a tendency to suppose that once a scientist has spoken there is an end to the matter, when what they are invoking might be seriously flawed. To illustrate we cite one of Dasgupta's criticisms of research by Edmundson on the effects of nutrition on work output:

> while calorie intakes were measured individually, energy outputs for each subject were calculated by multiplying the number of minutes spent on a particular activity by the group-averaged energy expenditure per minute on

that activity. Now this is something of an absurd thing to do, for there is no way to judge the work output for each individual per unit of time. Suppose you are ill-fed and hungry, and work at a lethargic pace for an hour. Your well-fed counterpart works for an hour too, but gets more done. Edmundson's technique of measuring energy outputs would attribute the same amount to both (Dasgupta, 1993, pp. 463)

These and other criticisms, Dasgupta argues, show that the apparent finding that output is not related to food intake is no finding at all. While examples like this—assuming Dasgupta's criticisms are themselves solid—are salutary, the aim of examining actual research should not be in general to carp and quibble (that is always possible) but to give people a keen sense of the extent to which we have to make the best of what is often a bad job in trying to understand the world around us.

Part of that bad job is often the social matrix in which scientific activity proceeds. Scientists are people like any others; they have their prejudices and vested interests; they have their networks of friends and funding agencies, their jealousies and even their philosophical leanings. They are not pure ratiocinators. In the more developed sciences what they do and what they aim to achieve are linked by vast ranges of theory and technical know-how. It may be tempting to give weight to all these factors and suggest that they determine the development of the sciences to the exclusion of testing against objective reality. But that would surely be to exaggerate a feature common to all activities. Many institutional activities have no external reference; their development is merely a matter of what has gone on in them previously and of relevant features of their social matrix. But cognitive endeavours do include, though they are not wholly exhausted by, an external reference, against which we aim to chart their successes and failures. The rivalry of competing players may here undermine any conspiracies to minimise external vulnerability.

RANKING IN THE ARTS

In the previous section we tried to show that in an area, science, in which most concerned people accept a broad ranking of what we have (for example, Einstein, as opposed to Newton), there are still devils in the detail. This, and the example of astrology given earlier, show that there are still philosophical and educational decisions to be made. In what follows concerning the arts, the immediate problem is not in clarifying detail but in presenting a view of ranking (value measurement) which is rationally defensible and therefore rationally acceptable. Here, if not there, it is the enterprise of ranking itself which is under question—and not just question, for many people simply assume that it cannot be done in any rational manner—rather than the minutiae of the results. In what follows we try to show that it can be done and how it might be done. But the broad brushstrokes called for here should not disguise the problems that remain even if our attempt is successful.

We have indicated in the previous chapter that appeal to the institutions of art reveals what the art world consists of, and presents us with the terms in which that world makes its evaluations. What we need, for our purposes, is an evaluation which we can both endorse and commend to other people. And, because what we are dealing with here is a curriculum fit for anyone within a given society, such a commendation has at least to stand the chance of rational acceptance. But this in turn means that the evaluation concerned has not to be a matter of simple preference but rather something that can be rationally defended.

Although this might seem to some an impossible task, it is worth keeping in mind the modesty of what is proposed. We are not concerned to argue the relative merits of Tolstoy or Dostoyevsky or Rembrandt or Raphael; comparative ranking at these levels of artistic achievement is fatuous. Rather, we are concerned to argue that it does make sense rationally to prefer Mozart to Salieri or Milton to Ogilby. There are two accounts of evaluation which would threaten such a task: Subjectivism and Particularism.

Subjectivism

Subjectivism can take many forms but for the sake of convenience we will content ourselves with dealing with what seems to be its most common manifestation. This is the notion, commonly met for instance among undergraduate students, that evaluation in the arts is a matter of simple preference by the individual concerned. So, for an individual to say that a work of art is good or interesting is really another way of saying that they like it or are interested in it. The only standards that there are or can be are the preferences or attitudes of individuals.

Before critically appraising such a position it is worth mentioning, in passing, a rather paradoxical but common assumption that often seems to characterise those that take up this position. That is a radical unwillingness to take the argument to its obvious conclusion. So, for instance, one meets such an argument when someone wishes to defend their practice of, say, listening to rock and roll rather than classical music, but when it is suggested that the argument—or typically, assertion—if valid also means that there are no objective standards within rock and roll, for example that the Spice Girls are just as good as Bruce Springsteen or Bob Marley, such a contention is often met with disbelief or derision. What this betokens, we suspect, is a willingness to deploy this type of argument to dismiss types of work outside the orbit of an individual's interests but a radical unwillingness to admit that the argument, if sound, also applies within the area of such interests.

Such a point may be noteworthy but it does not get us to the heart of the matter in question. This is the contention that, in the arts at least, the individual is the sole measure of value, and that liking and thinking good are the same thing. The first—counterintuitive—implication of this doctrine is that when people, including professional critics, *seem* to disagree concerning the evaluation of a work of art they are not really disagreeing nor are they really engaged in an argument over their seeming disagreement. If '*X* is good' in this context means simply 'I like *X*' then if someone says '*X* is bad' they are simply reporting their dislike, but such an exchange is no more a disagreement than if I say 'I like two sugars in my coffee' and someone else says 'I prefer no sugar'. But, of course, people do not usually stop there when talking about the arts. Indeed, there are differences of professional evaluation concerning individual works or particular artists which go on over decades and take up thousands of words of print. But if subjectivism is right, then it is difficult to see what is the content of such exercises. Given that there is no real disagreement, what are the participants in such a debate doing? They cannot be arguing—in any real sense of the word—for we usually do not feel compelled to offer reasons for our likings and dislikings, and in any case there is nothing to argue about. But critics, despite the contention of subjectivists, do seem to be arguing. Kitto (1956, Ch. 9), for instance, seems to be doing much more than simply reporting on his own attitude to the play when, in replying to a Freudian analysis of *Hamlet*, he says in effect that either *Hamlet* is a great play or it is not a great play. If it is the former then all of it has to contribute sensibly to its greatness. If the Freudian interpretation is correct then only a small part of the play is relevant to its greatness. Therefore, the Freudian analysis must be incorrect.

The second odd implication of subjectivism is that it rules out two linguistic moves which both seem to make sense and to have a substantive point. Thus we often confess to liking (say) songs, because of, for instance, their sentimental associations—we heard them when in love or in Paris for the first time; but at the same time we do not think them any good. And, conversely, we may think works of art good, for example some of Goya's darker etchings, and not like them at all. This half of the equation may be more problematic than the first, but such problems are not germane here. But if 'liking' and 'thinking good' are the same thing then such distinctions can have neither sense nor point.

Third, the truth of subjectivism would mean that it is impossible for the individual to make a mistake concerning the evaluation of a work of art. The notion of getting something wrong—or right—is the notion that there are standards independent of one's judgements whereby such judgements can be assessed. If all there is, as subjectivism claims, are the likings and dislikings themselves, then all talk of mistakes or correctness is empty. Of course, one's likings may change but change, in itself, is not enough to give purchase to the notion of a mistake.

It is worth emphasising how radical subjectivism would be concerning this point if the doctrine is true. Given that on that theory there are no standards independent of the individual's likings and the reports of these, then there can be no preconditions which make such likings and reports wise or unwise, shrewd or naïve, sensitive or insensitive, informed or uninformed. If this is all there is, then the tone deaf, the ill-sighted, the humourless, the superficial are just as well suited to judging music, paintings, comedies and tragedies as anyone else. Nor can experience play a part, for this would be to import something into the context apart from the likings themselves, and so the person who has little or no experience of a particular artist or genre will be just as competent or incompetent a critic as anyone else. Apart from the fact that such a person must be debarred from a whole vocabulary which is the commonplace of critical discourse— how could they possibly regard a work as original, fresh, surprising, shocking, banal, hackneyed?—this has profound implications not only for art criticism but also for education within the arts. If this is an area of human life where no independent standards can be applied to the individual's 'judgements', and the inverted commas simply indicate that talk of judgement within subjectivism is, at the best, honorific; if we cannot have coherent talk of shrewdness, discrimination, wisdom, experience and so on, then it is also impossible to talk of the individual becoming more shrewd, more discriminating, wiser, more experienced. If all 'judgements' are equal then it becomes impossible for some to be better than others. But if this is the case then it is impossible for the individual to become better at judging. If the idea of a mistake can find no purchase here then neither can the notion of progress. But if this is true then, as far as evaluation within the arts is concerned, the idea of an education within the arts becomes completely emptied of content. The exact nature of education is contentious: if it was not, we would not be engaged on our present task. However, we can envisage no conception of the term, and its associated terms 'teaching' and 'learning', which does not involve the possibility of progress. Education, teaching and learning all involve the idea of someone getting better at something. If such improvement is logically ruled out of court then with it goes the possibility of significantly talking of education and its associated activities with regard to the area in question.

The point can be made in a slightly different way. Teaching and learning involve someone, the teacher, trying to pass on their particular expertise and someone, the learner, trying to become more expert. But if everyone is, as subjectivism claims, equally expert (or rather if the notion of expertise has no place here) then obviously teaching and learning cannot go on.

None of the above arguments *prove* that subjectivism is wrong. As with most forms of scepticism, the determined subjectivist can maintain his or her position by insisting that our normal way of talking is in error and our normal practices without point. What the above arguments do show is that such subjectivism is a bleak, cheerless and counter-intuitive doctrine. And it is worth emphasising the last of these points again. Despite what the subjectivist says, we do *seem* to be surrounded by people and practices which *seem* to show that subjectivism is false. We do seem to come across different levels of expertise with regard to the arts and people do seem to embark upon and complete courses of action, for example, Literature and Fine Art degrees, wine and tea-tasting courses, architectural training, which they and others regard as improving (an awful word but pertinent here). It may be the case that all such activities are based upon a mistake. But it also may be the case that the subjectivist is rather like those who argue for the impossibility of translation between languages in a world full of bilinguals.

An interesting possibility here for subjectivism may be imported from economic choice theory. There it is argued by some that whereas a full-blooded subjectivism with regard to market choice, that is, the idea that what is valuable in the market place for individuals is simply what they do in fact value, is unsustainable because it rules out the possibility of mistake, nevertheless subjectivism can be saved by the idea of informed choice, that is, that what is valuable is what the informed individual would value (see O'Neill, 1998, Ch. 3). If we apply this to the arts and culture it does, at least, rescue some notion of, say, education within these areas. So, for instance, it would give us some reason for exposing people to the wide range of cultural goods on offer. But this, in itself, would surely not be enough. We would also have to endeavour to ensure that the individual was equipped to discriminate between such goods. It would be pointless, for example, to take someone to a wide variety of football matches, from games in the playground to World Cup finals, and to imagine that in so doing we have informed their choice, if we have not explained the rules and the point of the game. So as well as ensuring there is a wide range of goods on offer we also have to ensure that the individual is equipped to choose rationally between them. The problem here is, at least for the economic and cultural subjectivists, that it is not at all clear how this position differs, if it differs at all, from some kinds of objectivism, in that it does seem to give those that insist that there are standards independent of individual choice in both areas something to work with. And that is all the objectivist needs.

Particularism

There is another set of ideas which threaten the type of evaluation which is at the heart of our project and these are contained within a doctrine which we shall call 'particularism' (elsewhere called 'critical singularism'; see Dickie, 1997). This doctrine holds that because works of art are unique particulars, there is no possibility of reasonably comparing one with another, and therefore no possibility of rationally preferring one to another. The most that the critic can do, according to the particularists, is to direct our attention to the aesthetic qualities exemplified in any particular work. The keystone of this doctrine is the notion of the individual work's unique status, but it is just this idea which proves so difficult to explicate. So for instance, in terms of Bishop Butler's dictum that 'everything is what it is and not another thing' it is obviously the case that every work of art is unique. But then, in the light of this dictum, *every* thing is unique and, as the particularists do want to hold that there are areas of human life, such as morality and practical affairs, where rational comparison is possible, it cannot be this sense of 'unique' that is in question. It is exactly against such other areas of human life that the particularists measure art. Whereas, they hold, in morality and practical affairs generally we can talk about contending solutions to problems and rule-governed behaviour, and such talk does license different evaluations of solutions or behaviour, no such talk is possible with regard to works of art. They are not rule-governed and they are not solutions to problems, therefore there are no common criteria whereby one may be measured against another.

Whilst we think there is an important measure of truth in particularism, at this level it is both difficult to see what is being claimed and therefore difficult to evaluate such a claim. So, for instance, it becomes extremely important to look closely at the cited areas of comparison. It is certainly the case, for instance, that morality may have rules in a way that is alien to art, and that therefore, if you try to compare one with the other there are bound to be glaring differences. However, if one looks not at moral rules but at moral lives, then the differences between works of art and such lives may seem less extreme. It is surely the case, for instance, that a moral life is not made—usually, if at all—of a mere recitation and repetition of rule-governed behaviour. The way in which different lives may exemplify courage or kindness depends crucially upon the context and other content of such lives, and does not seem a great distance away from the way in which works of art may exemplify elegance or humour. Nor is it true that works of art have nothing to do with problem-solving. There is a whole range of arts from architecture through furniture design to flower arranging where it makes perfect sense to talk of solving problems with regard to both utility and context, for example churches are for something and have to occupy a suitable space somewhere. Even with regard to the fine arts—and some of these are not as fine as modern critical outlooks would have us think, for example because, like many of the paintings of the French neo-classical artist David, the works raise moral and political questions as well as aesthetic ones—there are times when talking of a problem being solved seems completely unforced. So, when Cézanne decided to abandon the use of classical perspective in his landscapes, it seems natural to talk of him grappling with the problem of how to depict depth without recourse to this particular technique.

There are other areas where rational choice seems perfectly possible between works of art. Museum curators and gallery owners are constantly in the business of making choices between the works of an individual artist or the works of different schools of art, and such choice can, rationally, be judged good or bad. It is exactly the possibility of judgement here which makes some exhibitions, such as the recent exhibition of Degas' work at the Tate Gallery, stunning in their achievement and some, even of good work, merely mundane.

Nor does there seem, at least with some works, a particular problem of the criteria for rational evaluation. In the Louvre there is a magnificent painting by Rembrandt of Bathsheba where the drawing of the left hand of the main figure—and Rembrandt is usually good with hands—would be a disgrace to a ten year-old child. The hand is far from vital to the overall effect of the painting (if it was, then the painting would not be magnificent). However, faced with this painting and one that was exactly similar except that this time the hand was dealt with in Rembrandt's usual way, it would surely be foolish to prefer the one with the botched hand to the other one.

Such comparisons and their soundness seem to be admitted by at least some of the particularists. So, for example, at the end of a paper where he has been arguing that comparisons in the arts are odious, Hampshire says 'if the judgement is an assessment of the particular excellences of works which are very similar, it might be enlightening and useful' (1954, p. 168) without seeming to realise that this admission undercuts his whole thesis. Of course, here it all turns upon what counts as very similar, but then this is a far cry from necessary uniqueness.

Gombrich (1977) has taught us that art feeds upon art: that artists face the world armed with schemata, conventions and traditions which enable them within their art to deal with this world. Nelson Goodman constantly reminded us, in the context of the discussion of representation, that works of art are more similar to other works of art than they are to anything else, for example landscape paintings are more similar to other landscape paintings than they are to landscapes (Goodman, 1976). If such insights are correct then it would be surprising—*contra* the particularists—if we could not measure at least some works of art against others.

There is one point of particularism which merits a different treatment to that given above. In protesting against the use of general criteria for assessing works of art the particularists point out, correctly, that a feature which may contribute to the value of one work may interfere with the value of another. So, for example, humour may be a contributing factor to the dramatic tension in one play but it may dissipate such tension in another play. Their conclusion is that we cannot use general qualities such as humour in our assessment of plays. However, this conclusion does not follow from their point. As Beardsley (1962) has shown, their argument actually disproves itself. For in citing the way in which humour may contribute to or interfere with dramatic tension such theorists are, in fact, using a general quality, dramatic tension, to make their point. All that really follows from their examples is that, in referring to general qualities, we have to be aware not merely of whether this particular work exemplifies such qualities, but also of how such qualities interact with one another in this work to affect the overall quality of the work.

The truth in particularism

Particularism comes about, we suspect, by ignoring certain features which typify the arts and by focusing upon one use of the word 'art'. We pointed out in our discussion of the institutional theory of art that many terms have both an evaluative and a descriptive usage, the first being when some assessment of quality is built into the use and the second where this is not so, that is, where it is perfectly possible to talk of bad works of art. If one merely insists upon using 'art' in the first way then comparisons between individual works must become much more difficult. Given that we are, within this stipulation of usage, only dealing with things that are good of their kind, we do seem to be forced into the uncomfortable position of ranking different kinds of goodness one against the other. (Think of the analogous situation in morality where we are asked not to assess virtue against vice but rather to assess particular virtues one against the other: for instance, is courage better or worse than kindness?) In such a situation it is little wonder that some theorists have thought that comparison is both pointless and invidious. However, if we insist, as we have, that both usages are appropriate in different contexts then this situation resolves itself. It does not take much experience of the art world to realise that there are a lot of very bad works of art out there. An acquaintance with amateur painting shows, pottery classes, children reciting their own poems, or the local pop-music radio station, should convince anyone that there are plenty of terrible landscapes, pots, sonnets and songs about. And these things are terrible measured against other landscapes, pots and so on. Even at a much higher level of achievement it would be a rare—and bad—critic who ranked Macleish above David as a history painter or Barbara Cartland above Jane Austen as a novelist. It is a feature of education in the arts at most levels that students are presented with only good works to consider; the choice made is between Marlowe and Webster and not between either one of these and the outpourings of the literary guild in the local parish hall. But such an emphasis upon the good does precisely hide the gulf of quality which exists between the best and the rest. And, in doing so, it gives impetus to doctrines such as particularism (and, possibly, subjectivism).

Once we get to certain levels of quality, comparisons between particular works do become difficult, if not impossible, and largely pointless. Why should anyone, for instance, be forced to choose between Keats and Eliot, Wren and Hawksmoor, Mozart and Beethoven? What would be the point of such a choice? Such a notion of choice becomes even more puzzling if what we are asked to compare is not good or great works of the same type but works of quality of different types: for instance, to be asked to compare cathedrals to concertos, or furniture to novels. Most of us upon being offered such a comparison would not even know where to begin; it would be like being asked to discuss the comparative merits of cricket bats and kangaroos. This is a truth within particularism and it is a very important truth for some aspects of education in the arts. It stops, for instance, silly questions such as: is Bob Dylan as good as Keats or Jackson Pollock as good as Rodin? If like can only be compared with like, then it may make perfect sense to compare the songs of Henry VIII, Schubert, Cole Porter and Bob Dylan (not necessarily for some assessment which leads to a league table but rather to see how each deals with the elements of their art) but it makes no sense to dismiss the last two of these because they do not write sonatas or symphonies.

Is there any possibility of comparing one type of art with another? Extremely tentatively we suggest there might be. It could be argued— although we are not going to do it—that although it makes no sense to compare architecture with music or poetry with painting, nevertheless there are minor and major arts. So, for instance, it does not seem completely crazy to regard pottery and the painting of miniatures as minor art forms compared to, say, sculpture and easel painting. The problem here, of course, is that even if we accept such a ranking this does not mean it is impossible to come across an exquisite piece of pottery and far prefer it—rationally—to an inept piece of sculpture.

If all this is correct, then certain points should be clear. First, certain types of evaluative comparison between works of art are possible and therefore our aim of promoting 'the best that has been thought and done' does make sense. Second, that although such comparisons are possible, they have to be handled with intelligence and sensitivity. Third, not all comparisons between art works are possible. This last point must cast doubt on any theory which seems to insist that such comparisons are possible, and this means any theory which tries to lump all works under one single criterion. Unfortunately, much aesthetic writing does just this and the urge to find, say, the 'beautiful' in all works of art does seem to imply that concertos might be compared to cathedrals.

Terms of evaluation

There are some terms we use to value works of art and culture which seem essentially aesthetic: terms such as elegant, tragic, harmonious, strident, witty, satirical, tuneful, dramatic, droll, garish, handsome. There are measures of evaluation, often of enormous importance, which although not aesthetic in themselves are used either to relate the aesthetic qualities of works one to another, or to place the individual work in its artistic or cultural context. So we talk of works being unified, complex, intense, fresh, surprising, original, shocking. But cultural artefacts do not merely exist in their own self-contained world, they often reach out and touch other aspects of our world. The most obvious case of this—although disputed by some—is works which engage with morality. There are formalists who would deny that moral content is a proper subject for artistic evaluation but it is very difficult to see how one could ignore the moral content of a Jane Austen novel, a Swift satire, a Pope poem or a Poussin painting, when coming to their evaluation. We also noted above that a wide range of works in architecture and design may be assessed, at least partially, in terms of their utility, that is, their fitness for purpose, so that the opportunities for worship that a church provides or the acoustics of an opera house may be vital grounds for evaluation. (A story is told of Frank Lloyd Wright that when clients complained that a house he had built for them leaked from the roof on to the dining table, he simply said 'Move the dining table'. But they were right to complain.) Any model of evaluation will have to take account of these facets of evaluation.

But before we consider such models it is worth taking a little time to consider radical disagreement about the use of the above terms. Such disagreement might take at least two forms. Someone might, for example, not be able to see the wit or eloquence or harmony of a particular work. It is certainly the case that we usually have to learn to notice such things and therefore, left without lessons, some people will fail to notice such things. Very often critical discourse simply acts to draw attention to such elements of the work in question. Most of us, with the right experience, the right teachers and efforts of application, do learn to notice what is, literally, in front of us. But some people do not; they will never see the humour of a joke, the tragedy of a play, the elegance of a painting. Should this worry us? No more, we suggest, than the fact that some people are red/green colour-blind should worry someone engaged upon a treatise concerning colour discrimination. The fact, for instance, that some people seem tone-deaf does not undermine the vocabulary or point of music criticism.

Such incapacities are to be pitied and not blamed. But what of the person who seems perfectly capable of noticing such things but refuses to esteem the qualities that we esteem: someone who, for instance, lauds the dull, banal and insipid over the vibrant, fresh and exciting? It is difficult to know what to say here, largely because such people are so rare that, if we did come across one, it would be difficult to take them seriously (what would we make of someone, faced with a choice of wines, who declared that they always favoured the thin, sour and musty?). If we did encounter such a person then we suspect that we would treat them as aberrant in the way in which we treat others as aberrant with regard to other aspects of life. David Hume, in his discussion concerning self-interest, gives an example of someone who chooses to step upon someone's bandaged, gouty foot rather than the hard cobbles (Hume, 1951, p. 53). His point, in using this example, is to show both that the theory of egoism throws up unlikely moral heroes and that such heroes need not affect our own moral estimations. Neither in this case, nor in the aesthetic cases above, has a mistake of reasoning been made. What is lacking in both cases is a normal sensibility. But just as we cannot cast our moral theories in terms of the grotesquely abnormal, we cannot do this with our aesthetic theories either.

A model for evaluation

So we need a model for evaluation which will, at least, deal with the complexities noted above. But it also has to be a model which does not offend against some of the other principles we have argued for. So, for example, it must not allow us to compare the incomparable. Unfortunately two of the obvious models on offer do so offend. Thus Monroe Beardsley's model, developed over many years, seems just too powerful to be of much use. For Beardsley (1958), artistic value has to be cashed in terms of aesthetic experience, that is, it is an instrumental theory. A work is good in so far as it is capable—and such a capacity does not have to be constantly realised—of generating a good aesthetic experience. Such experiences are good (another instrumentalism) in that they contribute to general well-being. Because, for Beardsley, it is aesthetic experience that is central, he rules out any consideration of, say, moral or cognitive qualities as part of the process of evaluation. Aesthetic experience, for Beardsley, as for others who use such a notion, is 'detached' from our everyday concerns and therefore detached from questions of morality and cognition.

If Beardsley's theory is right—and we oversimplify in the name of space—then an argument along the following lines can be constructed for any work of art:

P1 Aesthetic experiences of a fairly great magnitude are always good.

P2 If a work of art is capable of producing a good aesthetic experience then it is instrumentally good.

P3 This work of art can produce an aesthetic experience of fairly great magnitude.

P4 This work of art can produce a good aesthetic experience.

C This work of art is instrumentally good.

But the trouble with this is that the very elegance of the argument offends against the complexities of the area. For, if correct, such a model would allow us to disregard the non-aesthetic qualities of works of art, and to rank all works in a single scale. (Thus it might be possible with this theory to ask 'What is the best work of art in the world?') But neither of these things will do. It is simply impossible to ignore the moral dimension of some works. For instance, with something like Poussin's picture *Landscape with the Body of Phocion Carried out of Athens* our experience of the painting depends upon our knowing the moral elements of the story that Poussin is using. In the foreground the painting depicts two men bearing a corpse, unremarked by the people getting on with their everyday life, farming, getting married and so on, in the idealised city in the background. If this picture had been called *Plague, the First Victim* then the relationship between corpse and people would have been one of reality and innocence. However, given Poussin's source—a rather unlikely story by Seneca—what we have here is the body of someone who unstintingly served the Athenian state for fifty years only to be executed on trumped-up charges and forbidden burial on Athenian soil. With this scenario the gap between corpse and people is not one of knowledge but rather the chasm between injustice and callous indifference. Our knowledge of the story changes the way we see the picture and such knowledge is, at least partly, moral.

Nor will the single scale serve. It would be difficult enough to know what to do with the task of comparing, say, Poussin to Mondrian. The notion of comparing him to poets, architects or playwrights simply offends against the bounds of sense.

Nelson Goodman's theory falls to the same objection. It is another instrumentalist theory but here the key measure is not aesthetic experience but cognition. There are enormous problems in showing how all art works can be explicated in terms of knowledge but, even if this can be done, we are back with a theory that seems to end up by comparing the non-comparable (see Goodman, 1976; Dickie, 1997).

What is needed is a theory which has as large a scope as the above, that is, one that can deal with all works of art, but which is more modest in its outcomes. Such a theory has been proposed by George Dickie (1997). Dickie is, properly, suspicious of a unitary system of evaluation and, famously, suspicious of notions such as that of a unitary aesthetic attitude (Dickie, 1964; 1973). He proposes an instrumentalist theory, but one in which it is possible to include non-aesthetic criteria and where the types of comparison which are deemed puzzling above are simply not possible.

Dickie's starting point is to insist that we take each aesthetically valuable property of a work of art as it is and do not attempt to cash it in terms of some aesthetic meta-property. So, for example, elegance in a work of art is valuable simply because we happen to value the experience of elegance. Thus, we can produce a principle like the following:

> Elegance in a work of art is always (instrumentally) good in some degree.

However, we have to be aware of the possibility of both positive and negative interaction between the qualities of works. Elegance may intensify the overall quality or it may interfere with this quality. So we may have to reformulate the above to something like:

> Elegance in a work of art (in isolation from the other properties of the work) is always (instrumentally) good in some degree.

And, for disvalue:

> Garishness in a work of art (in isolation from the other properties in the work) is always (instrumentally) bad in some degree.

Where elements do interact Dickie believes we can treat such interaction as a further element of the work which can enter into evaluation. Thus, for instance, if a work has not only unity and elegance but unified elegance, then this may be important for evaluation.

Unlike Beardsley, Dickie also wants his theory to deal with non-aesthetic properties and he proposes principles such as the following to deal with such properties:

> Presenting a true proposition by means of a work of art (in isolation from the other properties) is always valuable;
> and:
> the approving representation in a work of art of anything valuable (morally or otherwise) (in isolation from the other properties) is always valuable.

Given principles such as these Dickie believes that one can draw up an evaluational matrix for any possible work. He writes:

> if the overall values of works of art are to be compared, it will apparently have to be done on the basis of the values of the particular, multiple properties of works of art. To simplify matters, I will consider only aesthetic properties. There are some *standard* aesthetic properties that all works have—for example, unity and complexity. All works can, therefore, be compared with regard to unity and complexity. Suppose that works A and B have only the valuable (aesthetic) properties of unity and complexity and that work A is more unified and more complex than B. In this case, it is possible to see that the overall value of A is greater than the overall value of B. Suppose, however, that works X and Y have only the aesthetic properties of unity and complexity and that work X is more unified than Y but that Y is more complex than X, then it is impossible to say which work has the greater overall value. So, even in the cases in which two works have the same two (or more) valuable properties and only those properties, it is sometimes possible but not generally possible to compare overall values. Of course, in the great bulk of cases, pairs of works do not share their valuable properties. Suppose work M is unified, complex, elegance [sic], and somber and work N is unified, complex, comic, and fast-paced; it will not be possible to compare the overall values of these two works—it will be an apples-and-oranges situation. Thus, in the great majority of the cases, it will not be possible to compare the overall values of works of art.
>
> In those cases in which comparisons of overall value can be made, such a comparison can be illustrated with the following comparison matrix for the case of works A and B discussed above. In this particular case, there were only two valuable properties—unity and complexity. Assume a scale of 1 to 3 in which 3 represents the greatest possible unity or complexity possible. Assume that work A has a unity ranking of 3 and a complexity ranking of 2 and that work B has a

unity ranking of 2 and a complexity ranking of 2. The following comparison matrix can be constructed.

(U3, C3)

(U3, C2)—(U2, C3)

(U2, C2)

(U2, C1)—(U1, C2)

(U1, C1)

Work *B* falls exactly in the middle of the comparison matrix and work *A* falls in the line above it to the left, which illustrates that work *A* is better overall than *B*. (This matrix represents all possible works that have just the valuable properties of unity and complexity when a 1-to-3 scale is used. Thus, some positions in the matrix may not represent actual works of art but only possible ones.) (1997, pp. 161–162, italics corrected from original)

Dickie shows how this approach can be extended to comprehend more relevant properties, but enough has been shown here to demonstrate the possibility we require. Dickie's matrices may look abstract and formal but at heart they are straightforward. The key to understanding here is to realise that in terms of aesthetic properties like can only be compared with like. Thus, for example, if we are concerned with the property of being funny, it is possible to compare the bearers of such a property, such as comic plays, and make a decision as to those that best exemplify the property. (Always remembering that it *may* not be possible to make comparisons across artistic types, for example to compare plays with paintings, and that at certain levels—both up *and* down—any attempt at ranking seems pointless.) It might be objected here that one cannot compare different types of humour, for example farce and satire. We may leave this as an open question; all that comparisons require is careful specification of the property in question. And it is worth remembering that often, for educational as well as other purposes, what we are concerned with need not be the overall ranking of works but rather the ranking of certain aspects of them. This is to say no more, for instance, than that if you are concerned with, say, the exemplary use of colour in painting, then it is better to look at works by Titian and Cézanne than works by Blake and Picasso.

It also might be thought that Dickie's admission in the last sentence of the first paragraph drives us much too near particularism. But it is to be remembered here that he is talking about the whole range of the different arts and that even if, in most cases, comparisons cannot be made—because it would involve comparing dissimilars—this leaves a vast number of cases where such comparisons are both possible and pertinent. It also may be the case that Dickie here is simply underestimating the amount of bad work that exists in the world. Dickie's theory is thus both more complex and more modest than either that of Beardsley or Goodman. It accords with our strictures against particularism—always remembering with many bad works that attempted features may have a score of zero—but also with the insights within particularism. It gives us some room to talk about the best (or at least, the better) without making such talk overly nebulous.

SERIOUSNESS

As we have seen, it is distinctly awkward to try to invert aesthetic values. But there is another challenge which is more worrying (see Brandon, 1980, for discussion of it in the context of morality). It is the reaction of those who exclaim 'why bother?' They do not think that ugliness is beauty but merely have no interest in making these discriminations.

One response might be to suggest that there are some things that are inescapable or pervasive—as has been argued with respect to architecture, we all need a roof over our heads; we all eat; nearly all make love—so it is mere prudence to have a concern for the quality of our involvements here. Life is fuller and richer if you have a garden to look at each morning and not merely a yard. The troubles with this sort of response are, however, that it does not obviously carry over to all the elements of high culture we would wish to include (what pervasive feature of life generates such a concern for epic poetry?), and that it is quite in order for people not to bother with refining everything they do. As Elliott (1986) argued, there can be too much stress on standards, and the standards may not be the most fruitful (Elliott instanced courtly love in this connection).

This latter point can be admitted, but it is not fatal. What we can say is that a certain amount of concern has been found in general to be worth its while. People do have notions of a richer and fuller life, of a poorer and more exiguous existence, and aesthetic concerns are typically part of the former, better package. And if not every concern need be manifest in every life, for example my enjoyment of literature means my garden goes to seed, this does not prevent us from allowing that there do exist standards even in areas in which we fail to apply them. People also reject too exclusive a concern here so that the lives of the members of the Bloomsbury Group (such as Virginia and Leonard Woolf or Lytton Strachey), with their all-consuming concern for art and personal relationships, seem exercises in affectation rather than in evaluation. (There are other views that take a less flattering view of human life generally, but they can only be sustained by appeal to unwarrantable claims about the super-natural.) A related, contingent psychological point is simply that people's tastes and proclivities differ. We remarked in the first chapter on Arnold's insensitivity to music. For such a person, it would be pointless to argue that they ought to take great efforts to deepen their understanding of music. This is no more than the point about colour-blindness we have already made.

Some thinkers have been impressed by what they believe to be an important contrast here between those activities that impinge on truth and those that do not. And certainly educational practice seems more willing to insist on 'the right answer' when simple truth is in question than when aesthetic standards are invoked. But invoking this type of contrast does not resolve the question—there is still an evaluation, that truth and its pursuit are paramount, and we are owed a reason for accepting it. We could follow Cicero in saying that a life can be distorted by too exclusive a preoccupation with truth or scholarship, just as it can by too much concern for gambling or fine wines. The Gellnerian point, that when we need to be serious we turn to science for the truth, is consistent with his other point that much of the time people do not need to be that serious. We can afford to let others worry about getting it right. So in general all we can do is present pictures of what seems a worthwhile range of concerns and hope that others will find them attractive, assuming they enjoy the resources required to make them viable. (For further elaboration of this approach, see Gingell, forthcoming.)

4

Popular Culture

POPULAR ARTS

The relationship between popular and high culture can be a fruitful one. Eliot, for one, saw the former as providing a ground and sometimes inspiration for the latter. It is certainly the case that one can with ease cite classical composers who have adapted popular or peasant tunes, writers who have transmitted the myths and fairy tales of childhood, painters who have transformed everyday scenes into great art and popular composers who have borrowed from Bach. However, the relationship between the two is, in general, not likely to exhibit the give and take of the above. Given that high culture is to be defined in terms of quality and that what is of outstanding quality *must* be differentiated from the ordinary, it is likely that such differentiation will be accompanied by suspicion, envy and jealousy on the side of those who produce or admire the ordinary and by snobbery, crass élitism and disdain on the side of the 'champions' of high culture. The position will be made worse by the fact that any reasonably impartial spectator of these culture wars will be struck by the relative ignorance displayed on both sides of the debate. So the supporters of the popular make no attempt to understand what they take to be the esoteric and those who defend high culture often seem simply ignorant of the popular. Such a lack of comprehension on both sides provides fertile ground for bad argument. This is bad enough when we are dealing with the value of disputed artefacts within a given art form or genre: for example, is Duchamp's *Fountain* junk or high art? Is Tennyson a great poet or an exploiter of Victorian sentimentality? But it becomes even worse when at stake are whole categories or genres of activity. Consider, for instance, whether the cinema can provide examples of high culture and, if it can, whether this includes or excludes the Western. In this area blanket judgements often seem to prevail.

Our task in this book is to defend and recommend a view of high culture, but it must be admitted that this task is not always made easier by those who seem to be our allies. The list of those who this century have defended high culture includes Eliot, the Leavises,

Bantock, Bloom and Scruton. But if one looks at the actual works of such figures the battles lost are as notable as the battles won and the misjudgement as striking as the fine discrimination.

So, for instance, Bantock and Scruton have both been inspired by F. R. and Q. D. Leavis's defence of the literature of 'felt life' and their espousal of 'moral seriousness'. And yet it is an obvious fact that F. R. Leavis's ire and considerable polemical ability were as much devoted to attacks upon professional rivals as upon the sentimental and the second rate (see, for example, the debate with Bateson in F. R. Leavis, 1968, Vol. 2, pp. 280–315). His reply to Snow's 'Two Cultures' thesis was a largely irrelevant attack upon Snow's ability as an author. His critical practice, although often incisive and sensitive, sometimes depended upon verbal sleight of hand and outright assertion (see Casey, 1966; F. R. Leavis, 1955). And, whilst a vigorous champion of those whose work he admired, such as the Metaphysical Poets and Hopkins, he was largely responsible for the neglect of whole traditions of English literature (for instance, the epic poem from Spencer through Milton on to Tennyson and Browning and the English non-realist novel as produced by writers such as Fielding, Sterne and Dickens) because such work did not fit neatly into his critical practices. The case for Leavis as a great critic is strong, but the case for him as a great critic with serious defects of literary and cultural vision is even stronger.

He shared a view of popular culture with his wife, Q. D. Leavis, the essence of which we can see in the following words:

> The training of the reader who spends his leisure in cinemas, looking through magazines and newspapers, listening to jazz music, does not merely fail to help him [with cultural development], it prevents him from normal development partly by providing him with a set of habits inimical to mental effort. (Q. D. Leavis, 1932, p. 224)

There is an argument lurking in the background here, but before we get to it, it is instructive to see the changes of cultural judgement which have taken place over the years in those influenced by this type of position.

The charge in the above quotation is clear—not only are the cinema, jazz and newspapers meaningless as bearers of serious cultural value but indulgence in such things will permanently impair your mental health. It is obvious to Bantock, in turn, that Chaplin and Eisenstein are film-makers of genius and that education—admittedly for the less able (although he does admit that the more able would be more capable at it)—can partly be based upon a discussion of film 'masterpieces' of the past, as well as the teaching of music beginning with 'skiffle' groups and partly based on the analysis of newspapers (Bantock, 1963).

For Scruton (1998) the cinema is an important modern art form, the twelve-bar blues may be significant culturally, and jazz, in the music of Ella Fitzgerald and Louis Armstrong, can be much loved and, in the music of Art Tatum, Charlie Parker and Thelonious Monk, is the source of 'spectacular' musicianship (1998, p. 93). Scruton's disdain has moved from the old targets to *avant garde* art and recent pop music.

What is going on here? How can the cultural demons of yesterday—whose very touch was polluting—become the heroes of today? It may be the case that a professional aesthetician, such as Scruton, is simply more careful in his judgements than his predecessors. Certainly, he tends to offer arguments for his dislikes in a way that you do not find in the broad, cultural comments of the Leavises and Bantock. But it is tempting to see in this change of judgement not a movement of sensibility but simply a movement of time: to conclude that what the Leavises and Bantock and Scruton are displaying—in their various evaluations—is fear and suspicion of new art-forms. Thus as jazz and the cinema become more familiar they also become more aesthetically acceptable. There may be the germs of a respectable argument here. It has been argued by Savile (1982) that the test of time is of enormous importance when we come to artistic evaluation. But time alone cannot do the job. To refuse, for instance, to read, look at or listen to works of art until they were, say, fifty years old would be both a frustrating and pointless procedure. How, for instance, would we ensure that the particular works lasted through that fifty years and how do we decide what is the appropriate time period? It cannot be mere survival in its literal sense that invokes the test of time, for example that a particular painting, score, poem is now fifty years old, but rather *critical* survival over the given period. So, for instance, we are in a better position to evaluate, say, the poetry of Eliot and Yeats now, than critics were when the poems were first produced, first because we now have a clearer idea of the works in their context, and second because they come associated with critical responses against which we can measure our own judgements. This may be right, but crucially it goes far beyond the simple test of time. And it does so because it involves judgements within the critical heritage which logically cannot invoke that test.

The conservative impulse to wait and see may be more sensible than a simple knee-jerk reaction either for or against a particular work or genre, but it carries with it cultural dangers of its own. It has threatened, and continues to threaten, as far as architecture is concerned, to turn a city like London into a museum of past architectural styles—of various value—rather than the vibrant scene of experimentation that it might be. In classical music it has led to a situation unparalleled in history where most contemporary interest in the genre is centred upon music of the past rather than on classical music of the present.

In any cultural field and despite the dangers, which are many, we have a duty to judge, as intelligently and sensitively as possible, what is going on now as well as what has gone on before. Such judgement inhabits a tradition which is probably more marked by error, stupidity and lack of sensitivity than anything else. So we, like our forebears, run the risk of such things. But the possibility of misjudgement can only be avoided by avoiding judgement altogether and that means giving up our interest in the art form in question.

We said earlier that there may be an argument that supports—or seems to support—the type of evaluation of popular culture made by Q. D. Leavis and Bantock. The argument, we think, goes thus:

P1 Works of high cultural value can only be produced by the very few.
P2 Such works can only be appreciated by the few.
P3 Therefore works that are appreciated by the many, that is, that are popular, cannot be works of high cultural value.

The strength of this argument, at least initially, seems to depend upon the status and strength of the premises. Let us, for the moment, take these as empirical generalisations. As such, P1 is true in the sense that great books, paintings, music or what have you, seem to occur rarely. (This premise could be made trivially true given a competitive definition of 'high', for example, 'what is better than the ordinary'.)

However, P2, as empirical generalisation, seems to be clearly false. If we take some minimally controversial works of high cultural value, for instance, the plays of Shakespeare, the music of Mozart, the operas of Verdi, the paintings of Rembrandt and Monet, the novels of Dickens, all of these were the occasion of popular acclaim. It just is the case that, in sixteenth-century England or eighteenth-century Vienna ordinary people who were interested in plays or music were just as enthusiastic about these works as the cultural élite were. It is also the case that what is popular at one time and place is often unpopular at another. Opera may be popular in Italy but not in England. Classical music may be a popular art form in Russia but not in France. Van Gogh, probably the most popular painter that the world has produced was, during his lifetime, almost completely unrecognised. But if the second premise fails then the whole argument falls to the ground and it does so because it confuses two distinct things: the artistic or cultural value of certain works and the perception of such value by the populace at large.

It might be objected here that our presentation of the argument is guilty of equivocation, since the 'appreciation' we mention in the second premise is different from the 'appreciation' cited in the conclusion. The first use of the term, it might be said, refers to the type of appreciation produced after critical analysis by a trained expert in the field, such as a literary critic or musicologist. The second refers simply to mass participation in the particular cultural event, such as going to the opera, reading the book. And one cannot assimilate the second to the first.

What we have here with this objection is a variation of a notion current in schools when we were studying Shakespeare and which is probably still current. Let us call it the 'groundling' argument. The idea is that, although there was a mass audience for Shakespeare's plays, such an audience was made up of two different sets of people. On the one hand, there were the discerning few who went to the plays because of the quality of the poetry and depth of characterisation, and on the other the groundlings who made up the mass of the audience, who, unable to appreciate the finer things, went for the story, jokes and violence. Transferred to the other examples we have given this means that the vast majority of the people who, say, listened to Mozart's operas in Vienna or read Dickens in Victorian London did not really understand what they were listening to or reading, but were entranced by the superficialities of the work, the tunes or the grotesque characters. Such a description, and the two levels of appreciation that follow from it, *may* be true. But they cannot simply be assumed to be true without further comment.

First, of course, it is the case that trained critics of whatever art form we are talking about are likely to be able to engage in, and articulate, their judgements of the form in ways that are not possible for the untrained. This simply follows from the meaning of 'training'. And it is certainly the case that the audience for Mozart, Dickens or Verdi were largely untrained. But what matters here, surely, is not whether such audiences were untrained—this is simply a function of the availability of training at the time—but whether they were capable of discrimination. In other words, was their participation really limited to the superficial or did it betoken a form of natural good taste which was simply, for contingent reasons, inarticulate? Such a question has enormous implications for education. And because the requisite training or education has been unavailable for most people most of the time, we may, at the moment, have no way of answering it. However, there may be some evidence—albeit indirect—for an optimistic rather than a pessimistic answer. So, for instance, if we take the participation of the audience in other cultural events, such as first-class football or cricket matches, such an audience is not, typically, ignorant and superficial. It may not, for example, be able to talk of the performances of its favoured team in terms of a theory of 'total' football or with the sophistication of C. L. R. James, but its knowledge and discrimination are often of a high order. We *suspect* that the same is true for a contemporary Russian audience of ballet or classical music or a contemporary Italian audience for opera.

Second, if the groundlings did go to Shakespeare for the jokes and the violence—and their counterparts elsewhere simply care about the tunes—they were displaying a remarkable level of stupidity. For it is an obvious fact that a large part of Shakespeare's work contains very few jokes and very little violence. The notion that a majority of audiences care only about the superficialities of particular performances—will Hamlet kill Claudius? Will Macbeth get away with his crimes? Will we be able to whistle the music?—runs into the inconvenient fact of repeated attendance which often typifies the members of these audiences. Such attendance can only be explained by factors which go beyond the types of reason usually given or by assuming a level of idiocy or childishness in the audience which seems inherently improbable.

One of the things which seems to unite the high cultural critics of popular culture—on the left such as Adorno, as well as on the right like Bantock—is their dislike of the commercialism which seems very often to be its *raison d'être*. There are long and learned discussions of the interrelationships of commerce and culture in the literature (see Middleton, 1990; Cracyk, 1996) which we cannot hope to reproduce here, but a few simple points are worth making for our purposes.

The first is that artistic production, on whatever level, has seldom been free of commercial pressures. We may find artists, such as Jane Austen, Vermeer or Van Gogh, whose relationship to the world of commerce was minimal or non-existent, but these are exceptions to the norm and any theory which wishes to treat them as paradigms of artistic production is simply forced to ignore most art. Artists, like everybody else, need to eat and, in order to do so, they usually have to sell their art in some way either in the market place or via patronage. Such selling may distort the art (Dostoyevsky had to lengthen *The Gambler* against his will because of his agreement with a publisher) but very often no such distortion is noticeable. We do not object to the works of Haydn, Rembrandt, Thackeray or Turner because they were produced, at least in part, for the artist to make a living. Nor is it clear what are the real alternatives to commerce here. The notion of state funding for anyone who *claims* to be an artist without judgement of the artistic product is an obvious non-starter. State patronage of recognised artists as, for instance, with the state funding of films in France and Australia, may be appropriate, but such patronage—like private patronage—may curtail or distort the process of production. For example, Australian films such as *Picnic at Hanging Rock* tend to be long on atmosphere and short on plot because the funding arrangements discourage long writing periods or plot conferences. (That the film in question exploited such economic constraints is beside the point.) Which leaves reliance on the market place.

But what matters within the market place is, surely, how the particular artist responds to it. Complete resistance is liable to leave them with an inability to produce art. Complete capitulation is liable to lead to the production of works of dubious value (although this is partly due to a lack of discrimination on the part of the audience). So, the only artistically sensible procedure is a compromise. The artist, to be successful—and here 'success' means being able to continue to create art—has to take the commercial world and its pressures as a necessary condition for the continued production of his or her art. That art can be produced in these conditions is shown by the lives of many of the artists mentioned above. That it can be produced in even the most materialistic and crass cultural contexts is shown by the example of the cinema. Bantock takes Eisenstein and Chaplin as examples of cinematic genius. The second, if not the first, was no stranger to commercial and popular success. If we look at the giants of film-making this century these would include the esoteric talents of Welles, Bergman and Resnais, but also the widely popular and commercially successful talents of studio artists, such as Hawkes, Capra, Hitchcock and Ford. And if a mindless commercialism produced sequel after sequel of popular—and sometimes good—films it was also probably responsible for the industry around Rembrandt which produced the hundreds of Rembrandt-type works which cause the task of authentication so many problems.

The area of popular art which is, without doubt, the area of greatest commercialisation is the music industry. It is also the area which has drawn the greatest dismissive wrath from the defenders of high culture. For Q. D. Leavis jazz was mind-numbing, for Adorno it was a 'filthy tide' with fascistic undertones (1973; 1976). For Scruton pop music is simply typified by hype and musical illiteracy (1998, Ch. 9). Again, we cannot enter into the heart of battle—a defence of popular music would take, at least, a whole book—but again a few points are worth making.

It is a simple mistake to believe, as Adorno seems to (but Scruton does not) that all popular music fits a single pattern: that one can lump Sydney Bechet, Charlie Parker, Elvis Presley, Bob Dylan and the Spice Girls together and dismiss them as a homogeneous group. These people are doing different things and such differences are overwhelmingly important in our evaluation of their work. To expect, for instance, that Parker would produce the lyricism of Bechet or that the Spice Girls show the folk roots of Dylan, is to show that you have not even begun the serious business of critical evaluation. Scruton partly realises this and is careful to distinguish the jazz artists he approves of from the rock artists he dislikes. However, when he comes to talk about modern rock (and it is a curious feature of his account that it is impossible to tell whether his strictures are supposed to apply to rock and roll from Elvis Presley onwards, or whether he is simply commenting upon the post-punk rock music of the last ten years) he does the same as Adorno on a smaller scale: he lists the *type* of offences committed by what he takes to be the *typical* rock song.

This will not do for several distinct, but related, reasons. The first of these is that it is a simple fallacy to imagine that what is typical of the whole is also typical of a part of the whole. Even if it is the case in general that rock songs tend to have qualities X, Y and Z, this does not mean that any particular song will exhibit these qualities. So, for instance, Scruton claims (1998, p. 91) that rock music lacks any significant structure. However, in whole sub-genres of rock, such as those derived from the blues, folk music, or country and western music, such structures are perfectly apparent.

Second, criticism of the arts, whatever the particular focus of that criticism in terms of genre, has to apply itself to the individual work. We have made it clear (see Chapter 3) that we do not accept the type of particularism which is sometimes urged upon criticism because, taken literally, this would leave the critic with nothing to say about the supposedly unique work. Critical reasoning, if it is to be reasoning at all, must make use of general categories of criticism. Nevertheless, it is how these general categories apply to this or that particular work which is the key critical question.

Lastly, rock music is an area in which the great majority of what is produced is driven by commercial considerations, where the question of sales has become a sufficient reason for production rather than a merely necessary condition which sits besides questions of quality. And these commercial considerations are focused upon a market which is driven by the choices of people between the ages of ten and twenty. Given this fact, it is hardly surprising that most of the rock music produced is lacking in any sophistication of the type that Scruton craves. Most fourteen year-olds, for example, either would not recognise the sophisticated if it stared them in the face, or if they did, would not consider it a point of merit. Scruton is right in general: most popular music of today is very bad. But then most poetry, painting and drama are very bad. The difference is that with such things this general badness acts as a screen to ensure that mostly the second and third rate never reach the public eye. With popular music there does not seem to be an equivalent filtering process. The real question here is whether among all this dross are some glints of real value. And whatever the ultimate answer to this question is, it is undoubtedly the case that some musicologists, whose credentials are beyond question even if their individual judgements may be in error, claim that such glints can be found. So, for instance, Wilfred Mellers (who, interestingly enough was a student at the Cambridge of Leavis and who worked for *Scrutiny*) has claimed that Bob Dylan is one of the most important song writers of the last century and that the music of the Beatles deserves serious musical consideration (1973; 1984). Richard Middleton was a founder of the journal *Popular Music* and in books such as *Pop Music and The Blues* (1972) and *Studying Popular Music* (1990) he makes a sustained and careful critical case for the worth of modern popular music. Such studies throw up problems of some general interest. So, for instance, there is argument amongst the musicologists as to the focus of critical attention with rock music. Is it, as with classical music, the score? Or is it, as with jazz, the performance? Or is it the record, as has been strongly argued by Cracyk (1996)? But such problems are the stuff of critical enquiry and the painstaking analyses of particular pieces of music that all these writers offer are its proper focus. Here, as everywhere else in the arts, judgement has to follow the offering of particular and detailed evaluations of particular objects. Anything else is simply less than judgement.

Because we are essentially concerned with what is valuable we have tried to avoid, as much as is possible, the type of sociological cultural analysis which talk of 'culture' often elicits. Such analysis is, of course, perfectly proper if we are focusing upon the anthropological use of the term but, all too often, it creeps, unacknowledged, from this use to the third use, where considerations of value in a substantive sense (i.e. where we are concerned with what is good not what this or that social group considers good) should be paramount. A crude example of this is the resistance in America by some students to the traditional curriculum because such a curriculum embodies the work of 'dead white males'. Now it is undoubtedly true that, say, Rembrandt and Mozart are dead and were white and male, but such truths contribute nothing to any discussion of the artistic value of their work. Wole Soyinka is black and alive but we cannot, from those facts alone, decide his stature as a poet or novelist. Often what is happening in such cases is an appeal to the over-simple conception of relevance which we discussed in Chapter 2. However, sometimes the matter goes deeper than this. If one regards the world from a more or less Marxist perspective where all history is history of the class struggle and where cultural matters are simply weapons in this particular war, then some such conflation of the political, social and artistic seems to make sense. What matters then is whether the work of any particular artist does or does not contribute to the coming revolution. And thus we get the aesthetics of Lukács (1964) which asks us seriously to choose between the work of Thomas Mann and Franz Kafka on the grounds of their revolutionary utility. Or we get the musicology of Adorno (1973; 1976) which tells us, again seriously, that we are to prefer the music of Schoenberg to that of Stravinsky because the latter merely recycles past musical conventions whilst the former breaks from them. Apart from the fact that such expositors of a Marxist aesthetic offer conflicting prescriptions (for Lukács modernist formal experimentation is politically bad while for Adorno it is politically good) it seems fairly easy—and often simply commonsensical—to resist such moves. If we reject the political analysis offered by such figures, and there seems little reason to accept it, then we do not have to choose between Kafka and Mann and we certainly do not have to assume, counter to all the evidence, that what is revolutionary in a musical sense must also be so in a political sense.

Even if we look at a more subtle form of cultural analysis, such as that of Raymond Williams (1981), where we are offered not the polar opposites of progressive/good, reactionary/bad but rather more shaded analysis in terms of 'residual', 'dominant', 'oppositional' and 'emergent' cultures, there seems little reason to believe that fixing a particular work within one or more of these categories will, at the same time, establish its value as painting or music or literature. And it is often very difficult, perhaps impossible, to position precisely individual works or individual artists. So, for instance, there are interesting and important points to be made about the changing art market in the nineteenth century and the way in which this influenced, say, the style of portraiture on offer. However, if we look at the work of, say, the Pre-Raphaelite painters gathered around Hunt, Rossetti and Millais, their work often seems to exhibit characteristics which are equally 'residual', 'dominant', 'oppositional' and 'emergent', but characterising them in any, or all, of these ways tells us nothing of their relative artistic status as painters compared to, for instance, Turner or Monet.

Whilst it is important to insist upon this modest version of the distinction between facts and values, such insistence cannot complete our discussion of popular culture. For this we have to look in more detail at some of the arguments advanced by the cultural warriors who are opposed to the cultural views of Leavis, Bantock and Scruton, but whose opposition rests upon very different grounds from our own. In the remainder of this section we shall examine two such views.

Janet Wolff's contribution to this debate is interesting, partly because it is taken as sociologically important and partly because it seems to incorporate some of the points made above. Her aim in

'Aesthetic Judgement and Sociological Analysis' (1982) and subsequent work is to present a challenge to aesthetics whereby art, its production, its creators and its assessors are necessarily demystified. Sociology of art has already, she claims, demonstrated that categories such as 'art', 'artist' and 'work of art' are 'specific, historical and arbitrary' by showing how these arose in particular historical circumstances in Western Europe. Her task is to show that the same is true of aesthetic judgement. The sociology of aesthetic judgement, she writes:

> draws attention to the specific social and institutional location of such judgement. Those who accord 'value' to works of art and cultural products are empowered to do so by particular social and power relationships in society, which situate them as critics and accreditors of art. They are to be found in establishments of higher education, departments of English Literature at universities, as reviewers and critics on certain prestigious journals, and as mediators or 'gate keepers' in publishing and the art market. The criticism of art and literature is thus executed by a specific sector of the population, with its own particular social origins, orientations and ideologies; in England at any rate, the class composition of this powerful minority is clearly unrepresentative of the population at large. (Wolff, 1982, reprinted in Sim, 1992, pp. 121–122)

But in challenging the practices of the above group she wants to avoid the mistakes made in the past. There have been, she argues, four approaches to the sociology of art/aesthetics:

(a) the segregationist approach, which simply separates sociology and aesthetic judgement;
(b) the reductionist approach, which collapses the aesthetic into the political or ideological;
(c) the transcendent approach, which makes (great) art rise above its social determination;
(d) the specificity approach which offers suggestions about the way we do discuss, or accord merit to, cultural products.

She rejects (a) because it fails to take into account the real contributions which sociology has made to understanding the arts. She suggests that the reductionist thrust of (b) is unsatisfactory because it simply fails to acknowledge the existence of 'aesthetic pleasure'—one might say aesthetic value—which seems independent of the part a work of art plays in the class struggle. With (c) she claims that the supporters of this position never explain, firstly, what 'transcendence' means, and second, the processes which enable great art to achieve such status. This leaves (d) as the only alternative that can provide an account of the 'persistence' of value across the variations of judgement associated with movements of time and space and which may explain the cross-cultural appeal of some art. This approach, which she gestures at rather than elucidates, will root itself in the type of 'discourse' theory associated with the work of Foucault. Indeed she thinks that Foucault in *The Archaeology of Knowledge* has already begun this task by talking about how space, distance, depth, colour, light and so on were 'considered, named, enunciated and conceptualised in a discursive practice' (1972, pp. 193–194). However, surprisingly and importantly for her own position, she thinks that discourse theory cannot engage with the problem of aesthetic pleasure, 'for this cannot be merely the effect of discourse' (Sim, 1992, pp. 129). She ends, again in a gestured rather than fully articulated manner, by suggesting that just as the judgements of science have been relativised within the sociology of knowledge, so critical judgements may also be relativised within the sociology of art.

It really is very difficult to see why Wolff's paper is thought to be important. It sets up a 'problem', which it never fully articulates or provides any evidence for, sketches out 'answers' to this 'problem' and then opts for one 'answer' even though, she admits, this 'answer' cannot deal with one of the key aspects of the problem. She then hopes that the sociology of art may approach the status of some theorists' conception of the sociology of knowledge. There is not one real argument throughout the paper and no real discussion of problems or solutions. Critically, no examples are given which show the relevance of sociology to either art or artistic criticism.

Let us put flesh on these bones. It is certainly the case that the 'criticism' of art and literature is undertaken by a specific sector of the population which is 'unrepresentative of the population at large'. But the same is true of judgements within science, mathematics, gardening and, of course, sociology. And this is not because of some kind of conspiracy within any of these judging groups to do down the general population, but rather because such groups claim—through dint of interest, acquaintance and study—to have superior knowledge concerning their particular field of judgement. It is surely neither surprising nor problematic that scientists, for instance, claim expertise in science and that their judgements concerning science are rather different from the judgements of the person in the street. If this was not so then we would have no determinate category 'scientist' and because of this nothing to study as *science*. The same is true with the arts. It may be that Wolff wishes to cast doubt upon the judgements of the art establishment; but such doubt cannot simply arise because they are talking about things they claim to know about whilst the general population do not. Such a claim to knowledge may be attacked but such an attack cannot merely consist in showing that the claimants are—because of the fact that they have actually studied the subject in hand—a minority of the population.

It is also the case that 'the class composition' of this minority is different from that of the population at large. But, in modern times at least, this is because a position within this minority is largely determined by a university education and such an education in itself is one of the determinants of class position. This does not mean that all the people within this minority derive from the same class prior to such an education and, although this is what Wolff seems to suggest, she offers no evidence at all in support of this suggestion.

However, despite the fact that, unsurprisingly, people who have studied art tend to be in a minority, and tend to claim expertise in their field of study, it is certainly not the case that such people speak with a single voice in their judgements of art. Within the art establishment the differences of judgement are as striking as the similarities. (Witness, for instance, the battles waged over the years concerning 'conceptual' and 'abstract' art and note that significant voices within the art establishment would, for instance, broadly echo the position of the population at large, for example with regard to Carl André's *Alternative VII*, the pile of bricks in the Tate.)

As far as Wolff's 'solution' to this non-problem goes, it too carries no real force. As she admits, discourse theory cannot in any real sense give an answer to the problem of aesthetic pleasure or value. What it might do, as it has done elsewhere, is sharpen our understanding of some of the particular alternatives on offer. So, for instance, discourse theory with regard to childbirth may be thought to offer a 'medical' model of pregnancy and birth and a competing 'natural' model. (Whether such conceptions are fully adequate is, for our present purposes, besides the point.) In a similar fashion a discourse theory of artistic criticism might include the moralisation of art offered by Tolstoy (1930) and an alternative formalism offered by, say, Fry (1926). What the discourse theory cannot do, in either case, is to tell us how to choose between those alternatives or whether the present alternatives exhaust the possibilities. Indeed, as has been noted by commentators on Foucault (C. Taylor, 1984), discourse theory leads to problems of choice which, in itself, it cannot resolve.

Lastly, Wolff's invocation of the sociology of knowledge as a model for the sociology of art is far from reassuring. It may remain the case that some sociologists still espouse the notion that truth is relative to social groups, that is, that what is 'true' for social group *A* is not 'true' for social group *B*, and that a similar position might be taken up with regard to value and art. But if this is so then such positions would seem to run counter to the state of the argument at the moment and do nothing to answer the key objections which have been raised against such a position. So, for instance, any attempt to define 'truth' or 'value' in relative terms along the lines that 'Truth' or 'Value' means Truth or Value for social group *S* simply re-presents us with the term to be defined and therefore takes us no further forward. Also, the relativist's claim, in both cases, seems to embody or entail a universalism which the claim itself tells us is impossible. So we may ask whether it is supposed to be absolutely true that all truth is relative. Likewise, we may wonder, with the value version of the claim, about the status of the mutual toleration which is thought to follow from the claim itself, that is, all values are relative to social groups and therefore we should exercise tolerance towards such values. The problems here may be presented in a way which precisely seems to undermine Wolff's position. If the objective status of art criticism is undermined by the fact that such criticism is made by a minority group, socially and historically located and unrepresentative of the population at large, then exactly the same point can be made about the judgements of sociologists. These too issue from a group of people who can make no claim to represent the general population. And if we should not be fooled by the claims to expertise made by the critics, why should we be fooled by the similar claims to expertise made by sociologists such as Wolff?

For Roger Taylor, like Wolff, it is art that is the problem and not popular culture. However, unlike Wolff, whose lack of concrete example seriously undermines her thesis, Taylor, in his book *Art, An Enemy of the People* (1978), bolsters his argument with a sustained, complex, and subtle examination of jazz and its relationships to art. Much of his analysis is compelling and in dealing with his arguments in the next few pages we are bound to over-simplify. However, whilst the story he tells is rich, multi-layered and perceptive, the conclusions he draws from this story are suspect.

The history of jazz, for Taylor, 'has been anti-European, anti-white, anti-bourgeois, anti-art' (1978, p. 155); this is both true of its origins in the brothels of New Orleans and in its spread to a wider, and largely white audience in the 1930s and 1940s.

In the first context, jazz presented itself as a 'disguised orgy' whose meaning was both affirmed and denied by the music. In the second, the reality of the jazz experience offered to mass audiences—whether in the dance hall or speak-easy—was undermined by the fact of the jam sessions which happened after the customers had gone. However, in both these cases—and Taylor is clear that this is not merely a case of commercialisation, for commercial pressures had been present from the very beginning—what we have is a music, rooted in the experiences of a black sub-class in the southern States of America, which is gradually but decisively appropriated by the bourgeoisie, in the form of both music promoters and music critics, and where such appropriation severs it from its roots. The music undergoing such a process becomes de-natured as it becomes more polite. To become acceptable to this wider audience the music, whilst pretending not to (because the feeling of revolt it offered was part of its appeal), must actually repudiate its roots.

The effect of this, according to Taylor, is most clearly articulated when he writes about a similar process happening to rock music in the 1960s. There, he says, art made a raid into popular culture and smiled upon some versions of it, but:

> Art is a badge of success within society, and to have it conferred on one's activities, when this is not normal, is to be inclined to bask in the value of the award, despite the fact that the total, social significance of awarding, in the society, is socially discriminatory against the mass of the people. To accept the award as high commendation is to accept, at the same time, that one's own life style is inferior. It is also possible that if the award is taken too seriously, it can suck the life out of what were previously vital activities. (1978, p. 57)

Some of this is true. 'Art' is, at least in part, an honorific term. Some awards are not worth having. And some do lead their recipients to repudiate their previous lifestyle. However, some of it is not. In the context of jazz, for instance, it is clear that whilst in some cases, for example Louis Armstrong, such a repudiation *may* have taken place, in others, such as Charlie Parker, or Chet Baker, it certainly did not. Nor is it the case that awards *per se* discriminate in an offensive way against the mass of the people. Of course, to get a prize is to be picked out from the mass. But such picking out is only offensive if such prizes are awarded unjustly, that is, in a way not relevant to the matter the prize is for. For someone to be singled out as above the average in a proper and appropriate manner is not, in any immoral way, to discriminate against those who do not win the award.

But there are further difficulties with Taylor's thesis. The argument is one concerning betrayal and loss, but with its emphasis on these aspects of the story it tends to ignore the other side. What we have with the growth of the respectability of jazz is not merely the later work of jazz men, such as Armstrong and Lester Young, but also the careers of Charlie Parker, Dizzy Gillespie, Billie Holiday, Gerry Mulligan, Miles Davis and many others. To point out that such figures have, in their music, moved away from their roots and leave it at this, is to do scant justice to the music itself. It may be, as Taylor claims, that jazz began as a music of protest but its musical peaks seem far from that beginning. Taylor seems, at times, to be rather like those followers of Bob Dylan who yelled 'Judas!' at his concerts because he decided to change his style.

The other very worrying feature of Taylor's account is that it seems structurally similar to other Marxist accounts of rather different phenomena which seem to carry an equivalent, and equally dubious, message. So, for instance, some Marxists, looking at the growth of the Mechanics' Institutes in the latter part of the nineteenth century, and the opportunities these offered for the education of some of the working class, have discerned a movement on the part of the bourgeoisie to neutralise the natural leaders of the working class by the offer of education and subsequent social advancement. The revolution is kept at bay by buying off those who might lead it. Such an account takes for granted, as does Taylor's, a Marxist view of history and its ramifications. Deny this view and one has substantially to redescribe the events in question. But more than this, the account, like Taylor's, is profoundly patronising to the actual people involved. It assumes, whether we are talking about artisans learning Latin or black musicians playing popular songs, that such people have a distorted view of their own and their class's interests; that *they* are guilty of bad faith or false consciousness whilst their proper path can only be discerned by the clear eye of the Marxist teller of their story. But again, there seems no reason to concur with this description or conclusion. And there seems good reason to demur. So, for instance, in the history of Association Football, where we do have a straightforward account of an attempt by the middle classes to impose their values on the working class, the workers did more than hold their own. Within thirty years of the foundation of the Football Association the working class had completely made it their own (see Thompson, 1988). To conclude, as Taylor does, that 'art is a value that the masses should resist' is to betray a view of the masses which sees them as enfeebled beyond recognition.

The view of popular culture, as seen from the right of the cultural spectrum, and art, as seen from the left, show similar features. Typically, there is a lack of specificity, the use of assertion rather than argument, the deployment of sweeping generalisations and the use of ideology to prejudge reality. The real work of the evaluation of cultural artefacts cannot be carried out in such a manner. Instead we need the detailed analysis, sympathetic understanding and willingness to revise previous judgement which should accompany any serious attempt at cultural evaluation. Until such a process is undertaken we cannot begin to fix the relationship between high and popular culture.

A QUESTION OF SPORT

Sport seems to occupy an anomalous place both within our culture and within our education system. If we take our first, anthropological, definition of 'culture' it is undoubtedly true that sport in general and some sports in particular are, for a very large number of people, a significant part of their lives. And if we look at indicators of interest, for instance money invested or media attention, sporting matters seem to be taken as important. A national newspaper, for example, of whatever intellectual status, is unimaginable without a sports section. Nor, despite the scorn of commentators such as Bantock, do most of us find it odd that intellectuals such as Gilbert Ryle and A. J. Ayer should have been as passionate concerning their sporting interests as they were about other aspects of their lives. It is also true that, following our third definition of culture, the one that emphasises quality of thought and action, questions of quality are easily discerned within a sporting context. It just is the case that Manchester United or Juventus are better football teams than their non-league partners in the game.

We suspect that Arnold would not have found it difficult to ignore sport. If the pursuit of high culture is the pursuit of the best in 'matters that most concern us', then sport may be ruled out on the ground that what it concerns is simply a game and that sport—or games—are, as Dearden has argued (1968), inherently trivial. However, although there is no mistake in arguing that the zeal and passion that millions of sports fans invest in their particular team or activity is all misplaced, that is, they may think such things important but they ought not to do so, it seems churlish simply to make this move and leave it at that. In cultural matters, as elsewhere, a simple dismissal of the preferences of a large mass of people does not get us very far.

As far as education is concerned, a large number of secondary schools, in Britain at least, set aside a considerable amount of time, for example a tenth of the school week, for participation in sports. Such participation is typically not viewed by the schools in question as a matter of simple relaxation, like break times, but as something to be at least encouraged and at most compelled. Even in our universities, time is usually set aside for the sporting activities of students, and such activities may be a matter of considerable interest for the university concerned. And things are of course much further developed in this direction in the USA.

Despite all this, a concern for sport sits oddly with our other cultural concerns and would be viewed askance by some cultural commentators. The gulf between science and the arts seems, and has been made, a proper focus of cultural interest, as in the debates between Arnold and Huxley, and Leavis and Snow, whereas it is difficult to imagine anyone making a fuss about the gulf between the pursuit of literature and the playing of rugby football. It may be the case, as has been suggested by C. L. R. James (1994), that this shows a significant difference between our culture and that, for instance, of classical Greece—there, the mass of the population, in Athens at least, saw no incompatibility between sitting through and enjoying the work of Euripides or Sophocles on one day and doing the same at the Games the next. But even if this is a matter of cultural shift, such a shift does have to be taken seriously. The problem, of course, for us if not for the Athenians, has to do with our second definition of culture. If we think, as most modern commentators do, that being 'cultured' presupposes some engagement with matters intellectual or artistic, then this gives scope for various concerns—one could be interested in history, literature and physics, but indifferent to painting and zoology—but an interest in sport seems to some, such as Bantock, at most a gratuitous extra, and for some writers an activity to be positively discouraged on moral grounds.

The morality of competitive sport

In a previous chapter we presented certain selection devices for the curriculum. One such device concerned the morally nasty. So, for instance, it might be the case that housebreaking was a feature of our culture in the anthropological sense, and it might also be the case that standards of excellence could be attached to different instances of the activity. But even if these things are true, few of us would think it reasonable to introduce it as a part of the curriculum in schools or recommend it as a constituent of high culture. It may be easy to see why housebreaking is immoral but it equally seems evident to some commentators over the last twenty years that the same is true of most sports. Thus, within philosophy of education, there has been a series of articles and chapters in books which have argued that competitive sport is morally tainted and, for this reason, deserves no place within our schools (see, for instance, Fielding, 1976; Kleinig, 1982).

Competition, according to this view, encourages a selfish or self-regarding attitude and nurtures 'suspicion, despair, greed, cunning, hatred, jealousy, pride, hardness of heart and fear' (Kleinig, 1982, p. 167). Such things are endemic within our society and encouraged by many of the practices within our schools, including the practice of competitive games. This encouragement and the practices that derive from it obstruct the co-operation which should be the mark of our relationships with other people. If this view is true then it is important enough to provide a justification for ending competitive sport in schools and—probably—for avoiding it in the wider world. But whether it is true or not partly depends upon the definition of 'competition' on offer. The usual definition taken as a starting point is that given by Dearden (1972).

The essence of Dearden's analysis is that two people are in competition if, and only if, there is some thing that they both want, it is not the case that both can gain possession of this thing and the knowledge that by gaining possession of this thing one of the people would deprive the other of it does not, or would not, deter either of the people from seeking it. Following this account, Dearden believes that it is not possible to compete against oneself, nor is it possible to compete for something, such as knowledge, which cannot be exclusively owned. Also, competition thus defined may not be inimical to co-operation but may actually involve and encourage co-operation, for instance in fixing and sticking to the rules of the game. As far as the first two points are concerned, Dearden may be technically correct but misses the thrust of some of the objectors. So, for example, it seems fairly easy to recast any talk about competing against oneself as talk about competing against one's previous performances. Whilst one may not be able to compete for knowledge, it seems perfectly possible to compete for some of the things which may improve access to knowledge, for instance a place in a university or good school, funds for education and the benign attention of one's teachers. However, it is with Dearden's third criterion that we get to the heart of the problem. Commenting upon the analysis, Kleinig argues that because Dearden fails to distinguish competition from other types of conflict situation his analysis is guilty of ideological contamination in that, first, it takes for granted that competition necessarily involves mutually agreed and mutually beneficial rules, when often this is simply not the case. Second, even when this is the case, it is not sufficient to establish co-operation, for that requires not merely shared rules but rather a harmony of ends which is normally absent from competitive situations. Third, Dearden fails to distinguish between competitive structures which we may find ourselves unwillingly inhabiting and 'acting competitively' which is the obvious focus in the case of sport.

Kleinig's points are well taken but, in the end, they do not add up to a more satisfying analysis than that of Dearden. The reason for this is that he, like Dearden, picks out elements of what is going on in competition without putting these together to form a complete picture. In order to achieve such a picture we need to attend to the different psychological levels which typically characterise participation in competitive sport. For the sake of simplicity let us, for the moment, simply concentrate upon voluntary participation in sports such as chess or bridge. One of the things to note here is, as Kleinig points out, that these activities are not just essentially competitive in that they involve winners and losers as part of their point, but also that their participants make this point their own and act competitively whilst enjoying the game. That is, they try to win and such trying must involve trying to make their opponents lose. Such rivalry is prevalent on the sports field and in the bridge club. However, to believe that this always, or often, breeds despair, greed, hatred, jealousy, pride, hardness of heart and fear (we accept suspicion and cunning) shows either a very careful but jaundiced selection of the available evidence or displays a very odd experience of, say, the cricket field and chess clubs. And the key here is to note that whilst trying to win is an important part of the competitors' motivation in these situations, it is *usually* not their primary motivation. That consists, very simply, of their desire to play the game. It is because such participants want to play football, or cricket, or bridge and want to play such things as well as they can, that they try to win. Anyone who has any significant experience of such things knows that one of the worst things that can happen is to be matched against someone who does not care how they play and therefore does not care if they win or not. Such a competitor does literally make the whole thing pointless. But what this means is that Kleinig is wrong both in his dismissal of co-operation within competition and in his highlighting of acting competitively as the chief bane of this type of competitive interaction. If the main aim of *most* competitors in *most* games is to have a good game then they do have to co-operate in this shared end, and a necessary part of such co-operation is acting as competitively as is appropriate. This last word is important: those competitors who go beyond this, for instance by cheating, are in fact ceasing to play the game because they are not obeying the rules which are constitutive of such a game. They are frustrating, rather than contributing to, the shared end. In this they are the mirror image of the person who plays but does not try. In team games, of course, such shared ends and thus co-operation must also operate at the level of the team. And again, if they do not, this tends to frustrate the point of the game.

The above is largely descriptive—although we believe that the description does recognisably capture the nature of many competitions—but it can be buttressed by some further points. The notion that such competitive situations are inhabited by a majority or vast number of people trying to 'win' by whatever means, such as cheating, can only be entertained by someone who believed that the competitive spirit, which is a proper part of these situations, is such that it routinely acts to impair the competitor's intelligence. This is so first because at whatever level of competition we are speaking about, it is an obvious fact that no one wins all the time and second, because if someone did care simply about winning—and nothing else—then this is fairly easy to ensure. Any moderately competent sportsman or game player can ensure 'success' by systematically playing only against much weaker opponents. The fact that we do not find the like of Omar Sharif playing at local bridge drives or Pete Sampras playing on municipal tennis courts says something about the commitment that such people have to the games they play and not merely to the possibility of winning. To compete with one's peers is, as any sensible person recognises, to run the risk of losing.

Neither the cheat, nor the lackadaisical, are welcome competitors in the type of competitive situation we are describing. And to believe that chess, soccer, bridge or any competitive game is typified by despair, greed, and so on, is both to misrepresent the typical and to display a frightening underestimation of most people's social and moral perceptiveness.

None of this is to deny that competitive games *may* be the occasion of such attitudes. But simply to point this out is similar to pointing out that making promises *may* lead to lying or marriage to adultery. It may also be the case that some individuals or groups of individuals use a background of rectitude to exploit their own potential. We have heard, for instance, of judo clubs where members are deliberately not entered in grading competitions so that, in inter-club competition, they have a distinct advantage, as the quality of their competitors is not matched by their own overt grade and therefore they are paired with people from other clubs who are likely to be of inferior quality. But such practices can only work against a background of rectitude and, even with such an example, those people taking advantage of the situation cannot take similar advantage when they compete among themselves.

We suspect that, for commentators such as Fielding and Kleinig, the real problem is not the types of situation outlined above. Despite the fact that their theories seem to demonise such innocent pastimes as bowls and croquet, this is not the real focus of their concern. Rather, it is the creeping of competitive motivation and behaviour from those areas in which it is, or may be thought, appropriate to those areas in which it is not, or is dubiously, appropriate. This, because it takes in the role of the market place in our lives and the manner in which resources are both created and distributed, is an extremely large and complex problem area. It is also an area which is not, and should not be, the focus of this book. However, a few simple points can be made in the present context.

First, if you are concerned with what is appropriate in a particular context, such a concern is not well served by totally damning a category of behaviour which in its proper context is perfectly innocent. If the discrimination of appropriateness is the point, then it is, perfectly innocent, and blanket condemnations hinder, rather than help, such discrimination. Here, tritely, it is those who remind participants in the type of competitions we have been concerned with that these are only games and are to be treated as such, who seem alert to the real gamut of human possibilities. And if sometimes our children—and people generally—forget this type of distinction it is manifestly the case that often they do not and that whilst those that do forget are real they are, thankfully, rare.

Second, both the defenders of competition and its detractors are both guilty of massively over-simplifying the nature of our social lives. It is certainly the case that competition enters all of our lives on occasion and that we may wonder whether its presence is either necessary or benign, but this does not mean that the whole of our lives is determined by competitive interactions—or co-operative ventures—and that our education systems have to be either resolutely for or against competition as such. The proper scope and limits of competition within the particularities of our lives has to be discovered by careful examination of these particularities. Without this we threaten to distort our understanding of these lives, and thus the lives themselves.

Sport and the aesthetic

It is possible to argue that we ought to reconceptualise at least some sports so that they take a more elevated place within our culture. James (1994), for instance, has argued that cricket should be regarded as an art. Although he recognises that cricket may be limited in range and subject matter, he believes that such limitations do not negate—and, perhaps, may enhance—other, more significant, aspects of the game. Thus, he draws attention to the dramatic qualities of cricket, both in the way that the game seems to utilise individuals like Grace or Lindwall as representatives of types, for example batsman and bowler, and in the way the elements of the game cohere in the whole. He writes, drawing on the work of Bernard Berenson, of the place of 'significant form' within the game and the way in which technique and style are the focus of attention when watching a great batsman or bowler. And he writes convincingly of the appeal of movement and tactile values and the ways in which the pull of the physical may exemplify itself in cricket as it may in sculpture.

It is certainly the case that watching a great footballer or cricketer at play is sometimes to be watching an impressive display of practical intelligence and imagination which resists any attempt to characterise it in terms of instinct or mere mechanical skill. The skill here is not that of the skilled mechanic or competent learner, but something more akin to the awe-inspiring skills of the great craftsmen or artists. Our response is not, 'How can *he* do that?' or 'How did he *learn* to do that?' but 'How can *anybody* do that?' We wonder at the possibility of thinking and acting so quickly, so incisively, with such grace and purpose.

However, despite this, and despite the passionate rhetoric of James' arguments, we suspect that the sceptic will remain unconvinced. He may implausibly suggest that James' arguments are to be regarded as mere sophistry and his descriptions as simple hyperbole. Or he may claim that to talk of a performance in cricket or football as 'intelligent' or 'imaginative' is simply a wilful misuse of such terms. A more pertinent objection is to point out, as David Best does (1985), that although the types of aesthetic response that James describes may be both accurate and proper for certain sporting performances, this does not alter the fact that such features of the types of game that he is concerned with are only contingently related to the games as such. Thus, it is unimaginable in the arts generally, and in some sports such as diving, ice dancing, or certain forms of gymnastics, for aesthetic considerations not to be our central concern. Without such considerations these and similar activities would lose all point. However, it is perfectly possible to come across examples of cricket or football which are perfectly of their type; they are proper games, played in a proper way, with a proper result, but which fail to exemplify any of the things that James wishes to highlight.[1]

The point can be made in a slightly different way, connecting to the moral dimension we have looked at earlier. It is certainly the case, despite the doubts of some commentators (see Dearden's chapter on 'Play', 1968), that instances of competitive sport may raise moral questions, say, with regard to fair play and justice. It is also the case that the players of such sports may exemplify virtues, such as courage, fortitude, determination, stoicism, dignity and magnanimity. But if these things may be true of particular instances, they may be completely missing in other instances. One may watch, for instance, schoolboys playing soccer and see little that deserves moral—or aesthetic—comment (but see the previous section for a possible qualification). Therefore any attempt to make morality the focus of our interest in sport is, in the end, doomed to failure.

Nor is this situation made any better by the fact that the study of sport seems to be finding a place within our universities. Just as the aesthetician and the moralist *may* find sporting examples pertinent, but also may not, so the psychology, sociology or physiology of sport may be interesting but they do not force us to reclassify the object of the interest nor to deny that the impetus for the interest, that is, the parent disciplines, goes far beyond this particular focus.

But are these points about aesthetics or morality any more than the distinction we made earlier with regard to art? If we take the notion of art descriptively, that is, to include both good and bad art, then, of course, there are examples of any art form which have no positive aesthetic quality. But it will not do to dismiss painting as such because the work of the local art club is lacking in quality. Similarly with morality: just because the features of a particular life leave us with nothing of moral interest to say does not mean that this life, given some slight differences, could not have moral import. All that is needed for James' case is that some sports can sometimes display things of aesthetic and moral worth.

All of this may be so, but in the end it may be beside the point. Even James, with his impassioned defence of the aesthetic in cricket—and it equally well could have been a defence of the moral or sociological aspects of the game—would be, we suspect, extremely unhappy if, as a consequence of such a defence, children at school or students at university were simply expected to write essays about the finer points of batting or slip-fielding or concern themselves with academic arguments on the relative merits of Hutton and Grace. What James seems to desire is not this, but that the participation in, and appreciation of, these games is taken as a serious and intelligent activity; that we do not characterise such things as mere mindless relaxation or vacuous entertainment; that sport, or at least some sports, regain their place as a significant human concern. But, if this is the aim, then it may be the case that the type of reclassification attempted by James is not the best way to realise it.

CONCLUSION

Competitive sport is not ruled out by its moral nature from being a part of educational provision. But such a conclusion does nothing to rule it in either. If we seek to do this, in the terms of this book, we have to return to the questions posed at the beginning of this discussion. Can we derive a concern for sport within education from a concern for high culture?

The first—and fairly modest—step here is to insist that there is nothing incompatible in having interests in both. The poet, musician, philosopher, scientist or what have you, who cares about how Tottenham Hotspur fare in the Premiership or whether England are winning the latest Test Match, is not betraying his calling or neglecting his cultural duties in doing so. Indeed, if James is even partly right, it may be that a breadth of interests which includes sport is a sign of the type of rounded personality which is to be welcomed.

Nor is it to be thought that sporting interests betoken a dubious desire for mere entertainment as a relaxation from the life of the mind. As James shows in his own work, and as attendance at any major sporting event will demonstrate, knowledge, discrimination and a sensitivity to the nuances and possibilities of the sport in question are qualities that often typify those who seriously follow such things. Indeed such qualities are more likely to be found in sporting venues than in the latest Monet exhibition. The idea that the person of culture must be differentiated from the oaf and the fool who participate in football or cricket simply does not accord with the facts as they are.

The next thing worth pointing out is that the institutions of education and the processes which characterise such institutions may serve many functions. Our argument overall is that the transmission of high culture should be central within such functions. But this does not mean that such a purpose cannot co-exist happily with other purposes. Barrow, for instance, has argued that the provision of opportunities for sporting activities within schools serves two utilitarian functions. First, it brings exposure to activities which, for an extremely large number of people, are productive of a great amount of pleasure. Second, at least for some, it inculcates habits to do with personal health and fitness which must be beneficial as far as the general health of the nation is concerned (see Barrow, 1981). Such arguments seem plausible, and if the second argument amounts to an appeal for social engineering it is surely of a fairly innocent kind. Also, sporting achievement is one of the areas of human excellence and thus the opportunities for such achievement may be important for those children at school who may fail to excel elsewhere. (And not only them, perhaps. For one of the authors of this book, one of the few things remembered with pride from his school reports was the comment, 'He provides the only fire that the scrum ever displays'.)

The joys and limitations of sport are well caught by Scruton when he writes:

> Of the greatest importance in our lives, therefore, are festive occasions, when we join with other people in doing purposeless things. Sport—and spectator sport in particular—provides a telling instance of this. Look back to the first flowering of our civilisation in ancient Greece, and you will find sport already in the centre of social life, a focus of loyalties, a rehearsal of military prowess and a pious tribute to the gods. Pindar wrote in praise of winners at the pan-Hellenic games. But his odes are not records of the fleeting victories of the various contestants. They are descriptions of the gods and their stories, invocations of the divine presence in a place and a time, and an exalted celebration of what it means to be a Hellene among Hellenes, sharing language, history, divinities and fate. They show us the spectator as another participant. His excited cheers, we recognise, are brought up from the very depths of his social being, as a contribution to the action and a kind of recreation of the religious sense. Where there is a true common culture, sport is always a central part of it; and the joyful abundance of religious feeling floods over the event: the gods too are present in the hippodrome, eagerly encouraging their favourites.
>
> A modern football match differs from the ancient chariot race in many ways, the most important being the lack of a religious focus. Nevertheless there are important analogies, most readily observable in the American case, with its great hulks fighting each other like armoured knights for every inch of the field, its roaring crowds in their Sabbath humour, its cheer-leaders bouncing and bobbing with choreographed movements and girlish shouts, its jazz groups and marching bands in uniform, its swirling banners and handheld vacillating flags. In such events we see a kind of collective exultation which is also an exaltation of the community of fans. There is, here, a near return to

that experience of membership which I described in Chapter 2, and even if the gods do not take part, you sense them rising in their graves, to peer with shy fascination from behind the screen of our forgetting.

The interest in sport is not yet an aesthetic interest: for there is the unpredictable outcome, the partisanship, the triumph and disaster, towards which all the action is subservient. But it is proximate to the aesthetic, just as it is proximate to the religious. The shared and festive exultation lifts the event high above the world of means, and endows it with a meaning. The game has some of the representational quality of the aesthetic object. It both is itself and stands for itself; once played it becomes a mythic narrative in the annals of the sport and a tale of heroes. The surplus of interest in the world which spills over in sport is the mark of rational beings, who are satisfied only by supremely useless things.

Still, there is something transient and unfulfilling in even the most exciting football match: the narrative of the match, the myth, can be repeated; but the match, once played, is gone. In aesthetic contemplation, however, we finally step out of the world of perishable things, and find the *unconsumable object*, which is a value in itself. Such things offer visions of the end of life, emancipated from the means. Some of these objects—landscapes, seascapes and skies—are found. But others are made—and when we make them we are consciously addressing what is most attentive, most searching and most responsive in our nature. When the aesthetic becomes a human goal, therefore, it situates itself of its own accord at the apex of our communicative efforts. We make objects replete with meaning, which present human life in its permanent aspect, through fictions and images that enable us to set aside our interests and take stock of the world. (Scruton, 1998, pp. 34–36)

Most of this may be accurate but it is still not quite right. Scruton, in the end, seems to want to dismiss sport because of the transitory nature of its objects. But there are other areas of aesthetic interest which are equally transitory. A compelling performance of a great play or symphony has its fleeting moment in time just as any football game does—and it could be argued that the more constant features of such things, the words or notes on the page, are there simply to provide the opportunity for such a performance—and with the games as with the play or music, we may keep the performance in mind long after the thing itself has gone. (With modern technology, of course, we can have lasting records of all three types.)

Surely the basic problem of sport lies elsewhere. It lies in the constant tension within some sports, such as football and cricket, between any aesthetic interest which may be provided by games and the essentially craft focus of the particular performances (craft/craft in our ugly neologism). Bad works of art at least always aspire to beauty, that is their point, but the good, perhaps even great sports player may simply aspire to win. There may be an elegance present in the play of, say, a Brian Lara, but the counter-balance is the dour efficiency of a Geoffrey Boycott. And the latter, in the end, in this type of competitive sport trumps the former. This type of distinction seems at the heart of Best's position when he contrasts the essentially aesthetic sports such as diving or gymnastics with those in which any aesthetic consideration is simply an added bonus. The type of aesthetic quality alluded to by James always threatens to be mere decoration; it may be there but it is always beside the point. The typical football spectator, say, exhibits none of the disinterestedness which has been thought to typify aesthetic contemplation. And the interest here is one which is external to the aesthetic features of any game, it is an interest in winning. (This may be what such writers as Fielding and Kleinig have in mind but the point we are making has to do with aesthetics rather than morality.)

One may make this distinction in a slightly different way. The armourer's craft was certainly elevated in Renaissance Italy to an art form and we may continue to admire the aesthetic features of a beautiful helmet. However here, as in the sports we are talking about, there is a clear order of subordination. It is the craft element with its drive towards efficiency which is clearly primary, and any aesthetic consideration derives from this. Beautiful helmets may have to look efficient, but if the look is all they have then they have failed in their essential purpose.

And, perhaps, this is really as far as we can go. Despite James' arguments, it does seem to be the case that high culture and sport fall on different sides of the fence. Whilst it is possible, and maybe even commendable, to be interested in both, one cannot spin the latter out of the former. And this means that there exists the possibility of being cultured—in our sense of the word—and entirely indifferent to the pleasures of sport. Given such a situation, but bearing in mind Barrow's arguments, it is probably the case that our schools at the moment are doing the right thing. There should be a provision for voluntary participation in sport and such sports as are provided should be taken seriously—for without this seriousness the pleasure inherent in participation will be lost—but no attempt should be made to suggest that this is, or can be subsumed under, the main purpose of the school.

NOTE

1. It is noteworthy that the type of aesthetically loaded sports which Best mentions are often the least interesting. Can anyone apart from participants really take synchronised swimming seriously?

5

How Not to Think About High Culture— A Rag-Bag of Examples

Defenders of high culture can be found invoking many and various allies. Many are, we think, out of place. These defences raise issues that we do not need to worry about or themselves create unnecessary difficulties for clarity of thought on these matters. In this chapter we will touch upon a number of such irrelevancies. We will begin by examining the assimilation of high culture to religion and religious concerns in the thought of Eliot and Scruton: this will allow us to indicate our stance on the place of religion in schools. We will then examine some psychological and sociological issues that Bantock has invoked in defending his secular vision of the role of culture, and conclude with Barrow's curious identification of culture with general intelligence.

CAN CULTURE SURVIVE THE BURIAL OF GOD?

Arnold was reverential towards religion and wanted certain aspects of religion to inform his culture of sweetness and light. By the time we get to Eliot (1948), religion in his thought has become central to culture, but in a way that perhaps alters what we normally think of as religion. His conclusion as to the part religion plays in culture is this:

> In order to apprehend the theory of religion and culture ... we have to try to avoid the two alternative errors: that of regarding religion and culture as two separate things between which there is a *relation*, and that of *identifying* religion and culture. I spoke at one point of the culture of a people as an *incarnation* of its religion; and while I am aware of the temerity of employing such an exalted term, I cannot think of any other which would convey so well the intention to avoid *relation* on the one hand and *identification* on the other. (1948, p. 33)

The notion of 'religion' used here is a curiously modern one for 1948, whereby anything that is valued within a culture *ipso facto* becomes part of the religion of that culture. That Eliot is committed to some such position—at least in this part of his argument—is shown by his examples on the previous page:

To ask whether the people have not a religion already, in which Derby Day and the dog track play their parts, is embarrassing; so is the suggestion that part of religion of the higher ecclesiastic is gaiters and the Athenaeum. It is inconvenient for Christians to find that as Christians they do not believe enough, and that on the other hand they, with everybody else, believe in too many things: yet this is a consequence of reflecting, that bishops are a part of English culture, and horses and dogs are a part of English religion. (1948, p. 32)

Eliot's ideas here are both interesting and important. It may be extremely fruitful, in examining the past, to ask what the religion of the time and place being studied demands and allows. Such a question when applied to modern Europe suggests connections, for instance, between the coming of Protestantism—at least in certain of its forms—and the growth of such seemingly diverse cultural practices as political liberalism and the sanctification of everyday life which we find in the paintings of Vermeer. However, whilst this may be one of the keys to past ages, it will not do for today. And it will not do because religion—in the normal sense of the word—has simply lost the overarching importance that it once had. So that whilst we may see the liberalisation of politics that took place in England in the period after 1650 as growing from the religious demands of the Puritans, no such connection between religion and most aspects of culture can be discerned in the present day. For the majority of people, in England this century, religion has ceased to be a significant part of their lives. And because they fail to look at their cultural practices through the prism of religion, such practices cannot be related to religion. Two things have produced this situation: first, the entirely successful attacks upon religious belief by the Enlightenment thinkers such as Hume and Kant, and second the massive indifference to religion on the part of the general population which appears with industrialisation and urbanisation. For some, religious doctrines have become simply unbelievable; for others—the majority—they simply do not matter. If we accept this as the current situation then Eliot's position above becomes one of equivocation. In a religious age, that is, one where Christianity is seen as the focus of life, we can strive to see the other cultural forms of that age as emanating from the form of the religion. However, in a non-religious age such forms can only be thought of as religious if, contrary to Eliot's declared intention, they are *identified* as religious simply because they are the bearers of the values of that particular age. In the first case, there is some, perhaps infinitely complex, causal relationship between religion and those things it affects. In the second, all value is defined as religious value.

The case is similar to the move made by some modern theologians. Despairing of the case for some more or less conventional Christian position vis-à-vis the deity, they simply deem anything of ultimate value to a particular person to be their god; thus, if you value money, that is your god, if art then that is. This, of course, makes us all religious, but only at the cost of emptying the notion of religion of any distinctive meaning, and thereby making the notion completely redundant. We will return to such matters in a moment.

If our diagnosis of the place of religion in modern culture is correct, that is, that it has very little place, then it may be the case that we are the first civilisation ever to face the future without the comforts and trials of religious belief. For Scruton (1998), for instance, God died with the Enlightenment but the burial has been somewhat delayed. He wonders whether, without the unifying force of a religion, culture will fragment and then lose its lustre. In not serving a religion it will come to serve nothing. But such fears may be groundless. If much of the high culture of Europe for the last two thousand years has subordinated itself to religious purposes, much of it has not and there is no real reason to suspect that the impulses of human beings to understand their world and to make art will not survive the cause they once served. With one enormously important cultural form, that of science, the liberation from theology was a necessary condition of its emergence as a cultural form, and the frame of mind that this emergence encouraged had much to do with the decline of religion. The scientist, engaged in his work, can proceed without any conception of serving God; but if scientific value is possible in a godless universe then this is also true of other values.

If this picture of the place of religion in our culture is correct, if the place of religion has shrunk from that of cultural dominance to that of being a private concern for a small minority of people, then the only debate worth having about religion and education is not *how* to teach religion in our schools but *whether* we should teach it at all. Such a debate was carried on over thirty years ago between Paul Hirst and D. Z. Phillips, and it is instructive to dwell for a moment on some features of the arguments presented.

Hirst (1974, reprinting an earlier paper) argued that since there were no generally accepted criteria for discerning either the meaning of religious utterances or the truth of religious claims, then religious education, at least as traditionally understood, should have no place within the state schooling system. In reply to these charges, Phillips (1970) argued that as far as the meaning of religious utterances was concerned, Hirst's position would entail that religious believers, when using religious language, would have to be seen as inhabiting the equivalent of a Tower of Babel, in which they seemed to speak but only in fact uttered meaningless noises. And this, Phillips believed, was an absurd position. As far as religious truth was concerned, Phillips held that Hirst had simply failed to understand the role of the religious community in determining such truth. It was not the individual, as Hirst supposed, that decided upon and used criteria for truth, but the community of religious language users. Thus, and this is a telling example, if an individual claimed to have a vision from God urging him to kill black people, the religious community would simply not accept this as a true religious claim.

Phillips buttressed his argument concerning meaning with an account of the meaning of religious utterances which he has since developed at length elsewhere (1976). This holds that statements such as 'Christ has risen' should not be taken as asserting factual claims which are either true or false, but rather as expressing attitudes and emotions which are conducive to religious practice. So, for instance, this statement might be interpreted as 'Let him be exalted' which is an expression of thanksgiving for the life of Christ and an exhortation to prayer. Any attempt to give a literal explanation to such statements, according to Phillips, results not in religion as properly understood, but in mere superstition.

Phillips' positions on meaning and truth are coherent. But their coherence is only bought at the expense of fatally undermining the religious discourse he seeks to defend and, in so doing, exposing the intellectual mess that modern Christianity finds itself in. So we could reinterpret what seem to be straightforwardly factual claims, for example, that Christ died on the cross and then rose from the dead, in a way that makes them purely expressive. They then seem to serve the function, among believers, that ritual handshakes serve for Freemasons. However, it is certainly not true that most Christians agree, or would agree, to such a reinterpretation. For them, it is the literal truth of the Resurrection which gives point to 'Let him be exalted'. But if this is so then the Tower of Babel scenario, which Phillips takes as a *reductio ad absurdum* of Hirst's position, must actually obtain, for when Phillips actually talks to such believers he is caught in a situation of systematic misunderstanding. This point could be made with other examples. It is simply not the case, *contra* Phillips, that when Roman Catholics claim that during the mass the wafer and wine literally become the body and blood of Christ, such a claim will be received as meaningful by most Protestants.

As far as religious truth is concerned, Phillips' doctrine both bypasses certain crucial problems and ends up in a conclusion that seems unacceptable. The problems are generated by Phillips' use of the religious community to solve the puzzle concerning truth criteria. For again, it is obvious both in a modern and historical setting that there is not one univocal religious community but rather many, mutually uncomprehending, religious communities. The differences, for instance, between the beliefs and practices of Quakers and those of the Roman Church are as striking as their similarities. In such a situation, Phillips either has to abandon the claim that there is one criterion of religious truth and support a thorough-going relativism concerning this matter, such as that Biblical stories of miracles are literally 'true' for fundamentalist Christians but not so for Phillips, or he has to show how such different truths can be reconciled. Even should he be able to solve this problem his conclusion faces further difficulties. First, it makes truth a function of orthodoxy because what is true is simply what the community as a whole takes to be true. This position should be decidedly uncomfortable for someone who seems to believe that most of what most Christians have believed for two thousand years is simply superstition. Second, Phillips' example is breathtaking in its historical naiveté. It may be the case—although we would not wager money on it being so—that no contemporary Christian church would accept as divinely inspired the task of killing black people. However, even a cursory glance at the history of Christianity reveals that, throughout the centuries, Christian churches have wholeheartedly endorsed equally repulsive 'visions'.

Phillips' defence of religion and religious education can thus be shown to be symptomatic of exactly those problems which Hirst claimed should take any attempt at teaching confessional religion out of the sphere of state education. And therefore Hirst's position— which is also essentially our position—still stands. State-supported schooling should not endorse any religious orientation.

That does not mean that religion and the religious life disappear from education without trace. We do have reason to learn about them, in what is fundamentally an anthropological way. In so saying, it must be clear that such dealing with religion is quite unlike the perspective adopted by schools on all the other subjects they teach. We suspect that few who endorse the distinction between teaching religion and teaching about religion are in fact prepared to stick to it.

When talking about Eliot's position at the beginning of this section, we drew the distinction between the position religion once had in culture and what it currently enjoys. Culture, in Western Europe, for most of the last two thousand years, has to be largely understood in religious terms. If we cease to have any understanding of such terms then our own cultural history, and many of the greatest achievements of that history, become lost to us. We are in exactly the same situation which faced an education based upon classical studies, when such an education was deemed irrelevant to the modern world. If we cease to understand the classical world and its influence throughout time, then we cease to understand our own history and we lose the possibility of appreciating the emblems of this history. The contemporary reinvigoration of classical studies within our schools may provide some prefiguration of what will become of the study of religion within such schools. The modern classicist is content with a completely atheistic stance towards her source material and seeks merely to understand the role of such deities within the culture of Greece and Rome. In so doing an understanding can form of all that which issued from these cultures. However, for all that the study of classical civilisation has been revitalised, it is still a fragile flower which may yet fail. And it may be the case that we are still too close to the end of the age of religion for us to hope that it can be studied now in a manner which emulates our study of the classical world.

A second reason for including teaching about religion arises from the urgent need to spread understanding among the different social groups belonging to quite different religious traditions that now compose our societies (cf. Mackenzie, 1998)—a context we shall be examining in more detail in the next chapter.

In opposition to our viewpoint it is sometimes suggested that religion provides something essential that cannot be given by a purely secular, naturalistic view of things. This raises the question, which provides our heading: would we have anything resembling high culture once we have reached such an awareness? We have already argued that high culture includes much more than serious meditations on death and suffering. Indeed, high culture is a deeply serious business. A secular naturalism does not avoid issues of death and suffering. It simply denies that these things can be invested with some sort of meaning by reference to a person or persons unknown; that our cries of indignation can actually be heard by anyone besides other humans. It need not suppose the possibility of some anodyne perfectibility to human nature; it can hold that our best ideals forever outrun our capacities as finite animals. Some perspectives are made untenable by such a naturalism, but they are not likely to include those that have given rise to canonical works of art. The *deus ex machina* has always been a grave fault in art and thought. Invoking it diminishes the value of reflective thought about the human situation, even for a believer.

LITERATURE AND CULTURE

Without doubt, one of the most formidable warriors on behalf of high culture was G. H. Bantock whose books and articles over twenty years were concerned to defend what he took to be the cultural high ground and attack the forces of 'progress' which threatened this ground. As we do, Bantock placed himself in the Arnoldian tradition but he used allies and armourers, such as Lawrence and Leavis, whose values we are far from endorsing.

Bantock's arguments were designed to preserve a particular academic tradition which he associated with the types of thing studied within universities and the grammar schools, partly because he saw such a tradition as embodying essential lessons for the moral life, and partly because he saw this tradition as under threat from the scientific and technological bias of the age. Throughout his work he insisted upon the value of the contemplative, and wished to defend this from the merely practical. However, in doing so, he distorted the scope and limits of both.

His account of culture—in the high sense—is contained in the following:

> A cultured man, let us agree, is a man who, among other qualities, has acquired certain elaborate civilised techniques, who has read ('read' implying with full imaginative response) certain complex works of literature or who has disciplined himself in certain modes of advanced inquiry. Now, even allowing for the pretension of those who maintain that there is still a good deal of undiscovered talent in our society, can it seriously be maintained that there is an unlimited supply of individuals who are capable of cultivation in the sense indicated above? To be more specific still, is there an unlimited supply of people who can respond to Eliot, Pope, Plato, Wittgenstein, Namier, Gibbon, Leavis, Coleridge—or any of these, who constitute a fairly arbitrary selection—no more than an evocative offering—of names within a limited number of disciplines but who represent the sort of level of understanding which the claim to be cultured in the sense that the nineteenth century was rightly concerned about would need for substantiation? (Bantock, 1973, p. 101)

Part of what is important in this extract, and in a way it typifies Bantock's work, is the difference between what is said and what is implied. What is said—note the last phrase of the first part—is that someone who has submitted themselves to the type of discipline which typifies university education, deserves the accolade of culture. However, what is implied—note the list of cultural icons—is that such a person must appreciate work in the realms of literature, history or philosophy. But even when this was first written in 1963, universities covered a far greater educational area than these subjects. Apart from departments of pure and applied science, there were the social sciences, the fine arts, and some applied arts. Elsewhere in higher education were studied such subjects as Fine Art, Design, Graphics, Pottery and so on. Given this type of list Bantock's ideas of cultural engagement seem rather limited. If one does produce a list of cultural icons more representative of high culture than those of Bantock—but necessarily still limited—which might include Einstein, Mozart, Turner, Brunel, Adam, Wren, Chippendale, Moore, Darwin, Boole, Britten, Lister, Gibbon and Wedgewood, the possibilities of cultural engagement, at the highest level, seem much more open than Bantock seems to imply. And the possibility that there is, in the general population, not an 'unlimited' (that is simply hyperbole) but a very large number who could benefit from such engagement but do not get the chance to do so, becomes a very credible claim.

One of the points of Snow's lecture on the two cultures which Leavis and Bantock never take seriously is his insistence that, in the modern age, a failure to understand and appreciate science is far more damning culturally than a failure to understand and appreciate, say, Lawrence. So, whilst Leavis is quite happy to tear to pieces—altogether unfairly—Snow's claims to literary understanding, he is never prepared to defend his own position as far as the understanding of science is concerned. Science, typically, is presented as something concerned with grubby practicalities, as opposed to the disinterested contemplation which typifies a proper concern for literature. What is lost, with just this one move, is the sense of awe and wonder which we find in the work of the great scientists and mathematicians.

The reason for this curiously circumscribed view of high culture is easy to find if we look deeper into the position of Leavis and Bantock. The type of cultural engagement which Bantock sees in the work of Leavis and which appears to him to be the *sine qua non* of educated cultivation is a concern for 'felt life' which is evidenced by the greatest poets and novelists and which manifests itself in an emotional and intellectual grasp of particularities. The critics, in their turn, respond by entering empathetically into such a concern and showing how its different aspects are related. Bantock, quoting Leavis, sees the following passage as encapsulating this 'method':

> The critic—the reader of poetry—is indeed concerned with evaluation, but to figure him as measuring with a norm which he brings up to the object and applies from the outside is to misrepresent the process. The critic's aim is, first, to realise as sensitively and completely as possible this or that which claims his attention; and a certain valuing is implicit in the realising. As he matures in experience of the new thing he asks explicitly and implicitly: 'Where does this come? How does it stand in relation to. . . .? How relatively important does it seem?' And the organisation into which it settles as a constituent in becoming 'placed' is an organisation of similarly placed things, things that have found their bearings with regard to one another, and not a theoretical system or a system determined by abstract considerations. (Leavis, *The Common Pursuit*, p. 213, quoted in Bantock, 1973, p. 159)

This attention to the particular on the part of both the artist and the critic, with its echoes of the work of the later Wittgenstein, goes far beyond the merely artistic. For both Bantock and Leavis it is a moral concern which encapsulates the essence of spiritual and moral health.

It is obvious that the types of claim made here may be extremely important for critical practice. It is also obvious that a full examination of them is far beyond the scope of this book. However, some points do need making. First, if it is the conscious application of such sensibility that makes 'the cultured' then Bantock's earlier claims that culture can also be exhibited by participation in the developed university disciplines seem distinctly odd. If this type of procedure is the essence of culture then it is the case that physicists, sociologists, historians, engineers, botanists and philosophers are not, by and large, cultured. If on the other hand this is merely one way of exemplifying culture—and therefore one way of being spiritually and morally healthy—then why give it the prominence that Bantock does? The suspicion is that although it is the latter claim that is explicitly endorsed, it is the former that is the heart of Bantock's argument. But then, if this is so, being cultured has nothing to do with appreciation and understanding of a wide range of cultural activities and everything to do with approaching a certain type of literature in a certain way. Such a claim seems manifestly absurd and, if it really is what Bantock means, it would need a far more robust and detailed defence than he ever attempts.

Second, what Bantock is endorsing here are the disputed claims of a particular literary theorist. Even if we allow Leavis an eminent place in modern critical theory and think that the objects of his critical adulation are worthy of such praise—and would anyone deny this of Donne, Hopkins, Shakespeare, Austen, James, Conrad?—it is still widely acknowledged that not all literature works in the ways that Leavis was concerned to champion and that the job of the critic has to go beyond the Leavisite procedure. It is notorious, for instance, that there are whole traditions within English literature which Leavis seriously undervalued—traditions in poetry associated with Spencer, Milton and Tennyson and in the novel with Fielding, Smollett, Thackeray and Dickens. (The judgement which Leavis advances in *The Great Tradition*, that of all Dickens' work only *Hard Times* is morally serious, today simply appears laughable.) It is equally notorious that, whatever the quality of D. H. Lawrence's novels, the claims made for him by Leavis are inflated almost beyond belief. If we do insist, as we should, that at most Leavis offers us partial insights into a part of English literature—and a very small part of English culture—then we have every reason to doubt Bantock's use of him as a guide to culture and cultural education.

As to the claim, made very explicitly by Leavis and with a little more caution by Bantock, that what we have in, say, the novels of Lawrence is not merely an awareness of 'felt life' but an insight into what it is to be spiritually and morally healthy, this would only be entertained by those who have lost all sense of the proper meanings of 'spiritual' and 'moral'. (For an elucidation of this point and a critical, but generous, assessment of Leavis' work, see Casey, 1966.)

CLASS

At times Bantock writes like an embattled educationalist trying to ensure two laudable aims. The first is the education of our brightest children, from whatever background, who he fears may be lost in the comprehensive system. The second is a worthwhile education for our less bright children. We think him wrong in both outline and detail in his prescriptions for these two groups, but no serious educationalist could wonder whether his basic concerns are honourable.

However, at times Bantock writes like the most rabid of class warriors determined to stem the tide of the great unwashed. Thus he quotes, with seeming approval, Lawrence's words: 'The great mass of humanity should never learn to read and write—never!' (*Fantasia of the Unconscious*, cited in Bantock, 1967, p. 111). And he begins a section of another book with some of Lawrence's suggestions for the education of the people: 'the rudiments of domestic labour, such as boat mending, plumbing, soldering, painting and paper hanging, gardening... all these minor trades on which domestic life depends, and in which every working man should have some proficiency' ('Education of the People', cited in Bantock, 1973, p. 217).

He is perfectly capable, whilst discussing the work of Raymond Williams and Richard Hoggart, of accusing them of failure because they simultaneously adhere to the cultural ideals of the minority whilst also pledging their allegiance to the majority group, that is, the working class, 'whose own positive qualitative contribution [to our culture] has been minimal within the industrial period' (Bantock, 1967, p. 160). This leads Williams and Hoggart, according to Bantock, 'to overstress the contribution that ordinary people make to the sustaining of our culture' (1967, p. 160).

In a short essay on the curriculum, Bantock brings in not one but three theories of educational psychology to explain why the masses cannot benefit from his highest educational ideals (Bantock, 1971, pp. 251–264). It little seems to matter to him that the three theories— Jensen's IQ theory, Bernstein's linguistic deficit theory and the work of Piaget—are in fact answers to rather different questions and may be incompatible with one another, or that his use of Piaget to assert that the majority of children at secondary school only reach the concrete operational level of thought might, if true, debar such children from the study of pure mathematics or science, but would do nothing to hinder them from focusing in Leavis' preferred way on the particularities revealed in literature.

Bantock's attitude to the working class is usually affectionate; his concern for working-class education seems real. However, the whole tenor of his approach is patronising in the extreme. He tends not to talk of the working class but of 'the folk' and he seems to relate their particular educational problems, at least partly, to the demand for universal literacy which accompanied the industrial revolution and disrupted their largely oral traditions. (Although it is never made at all clear how the fact that our great great grandfathers might not have been able to read should affect the educability and cultural deserts of anyone now!) As always with Bantock, in the background one can hear the voice of the Leavises. In this particular case it is Q.D., rather than F.R., who wrote of 'the folk':

> But these [ordinary folk in past days] had a real social life, they had a way of living that obeyed the natural rhythm and furnished them genuine and what might be called, to borrow a word from the copywriter, 'creative' interests...country arts, traditional crafts and games and singing. (Q. D. Leavis, 1932, p. 209)

Bantock sometimes writes in this vein and he certainly saw it as part of his task to suggest educational provision which would create a new folk culture. However both his and Leavis' description of the situation of 'the folk' in early or pre-industrial society is deeply flawed and the traditions he wished somehow to reinvent probably never existed in any general way.

That the description is false can easily be gleaned from contemporary sources, such as Disraeli's *Sybil, or the Two Nations* where, for instance, the town of Marney is described (Book II, Chapter 3) or from the novels and journalism of Thomas Hardy. If we look as well at one of the best social histories of the nineteenth century, Thompson's *The Rise of Respectable Society*, we find that the lot of the rural worker throughout that century in terms of work, housing, leisure and cultural activities remained appalling and that it is likely that it was only the increased opportunities for work in the towns which made countryside employers improve their treatment of their employees and thus made their lives 'less miserable and wretched than their predecessors of the 1830s' (Thompson, 1988, p. 240). The 'creativity' talked of by Leavis had little scope for its expression in lives in which six-day working for full daylight hours was expected and in which Sunday was, quite literally, a necessary day of rest. Any leisure hours were just as likely to involve cock- or dog-fighting as indulgence in rustic crafts.

The Bantock/Leavis conception of the previous idyll of 'the folk' is the purest romantic nonsense. And their notion of the degradation that was suffered when these 'folk' moved into the industrial towns is also dangerous nonsense. It is certainly the case that workers in Glasgow, Manchester and Leeds might live in unsanitary, crowded and dangerous slums with little chance of worthwhile cultural activity, but often the housing they left in the countryside was little better and was attended with burdensome restrictions on their personal freedom. But again they might instead live in decent houses provided by enlightened employers, such as Titus Salt, and be given real opportunities for education and culture by such men. So, for instance, some employers provided libraries and reading rooms and means of cultural expression.

So what is one to make of the suggestion of Bantock above that the contribution of the working classes to culture has, in the industrial era, been minimal? Certainly, some of Bantock's antagonists take this charge seriously and try to rebut it (see Entwistle, 1978, Chs. 3–5). But they fail to register that the charge itself is either distinctly odd and false, or alternatively true but trivially so. Thus, if we take the charge to be against the working class as a class, then the charge is odd. And it is so because we do not usually expect social classes qua social classes to contribute collectively to culture in any significant way. What would we, for instance, make of the statement that the petty bourgeoisie as a class had—or had not—made such a significant contribution to culture? However, if we do accept the collectivist interpretation of the statement, the working class, as a matter of fact, comes out rather well. So, for instance, three significant musical forms of the modern period—jazz, brass band music, and rock and roll—all derive from working-class activities. Association football, although not originally a working-class sport (see Thompson, 1988, pp. 296–297) owes its modern form and popularity to the working class. And if, as Entwistle insists that we do, we include in our notion of culture forms of political organisation then the modern world has been transformed by working-class activity. None of this is to deny the fact that, during the same period, it is the middle class and above who sustain some of the elements of traditional culture (opera, poetry, painting); but sustenance is not the same as origination.

On the other hand, if we take Bantock's claim, rather more naturally, to be not about classes as such, but rather about individuals within classes, then, in the light of what he says above concerning 'ordinary people' the claim *must be* trivially true. This is necessarily the case because anyone who does make a positive contribution to culture becomes, by definition, not ordinary. However, if we forget the final cultural status of individuals and look at their class origins, it is at least arguable that the list of working-class cultural heroes is significant. Depending how we precisely define 'working class' it might, over the last three hundred years, include Gainsborough, Blake and Turner, the Stephensons and Brunel, Clare, Dickens and Lawrence—a not inconsiderable list. The position is complicated, of course, by the fact that whatever the humble origins of such people they tend, by dint of public recognition, to end up far from such origins. This becomes even more true with the advent of universal secondary education and the expansion of university provision. Any discussion of class and culture over the last fifty years must bear in mind—but often does not—the fact that, in this period, entry into cultural significance is usually via the portals of the universities, and that, whatever the class origin of university students, the mere fact of crossing such portals makes them, at a step, middle class.

This also bears upon Bantock's use of psychology and his seeming endorsement of some of Lawrence's more wicked recommendations for education. If, as is now the case, approximately a third of the British university undergraduate population derives originally from the working class then Bantock's use of psychological theory becomes self-refuting. Even if we accept some, or all, of the theories he cites (and this is a very large 'if': see Winch, 1990) the scope of such theories is such that they are, for the practical purpose of introducing pupils to culture, more or less useless. Given the statistic above about working-class success, this must mean that a significant proportion of this class rises above the general strictures of Jensen, Bernstein or Piaget, and manages perfectly well at studies that involve abstraction or elaborated codes or what have you. But this in turn means that, given a class—or school—of working-class children we cannot know, in advance of trying, whether such children can be brought to engage successfully with high culture (however one defines this). To assume, as Lawrence seems to do, that such children must necessarily fail or that what they need, *pace* Bantock, is an altogether different education, is simply to ignore the logic of the situation.

SOCIOLOGICAL INTERLUDE

Bantock proposed psychological obstacles to the thoroughgoing democratisation of high culture. Crudely speaking, too many people are supposed to be incapable (as a brute psychological fact) of the type of profoundly literate thought and activity which it requires. We have indicated that we think there is absolutely no reason to accept this pessimistic prognosis. That might seem to be the end of the matter.

But, as Bantock's use of the early Bernstein might suggest, there is another way of erecting obstacles to the extension of high culture—through appeal to sociological findings. The thought would then be, not that too many people simply do not have the required intellectual equipment, but that too many people will find themselves in socio-economic relations that preclude their engagement in high culture. So long as people are distinguished by economic class, so long will different cultural forms be used by them: as badges of identity, as ways of distinguishing themselves from groups below and above them, as ways of displaying their relative standing and dependence on others. These are not simply explicit, conscious decisions that might easily be changed by taking thought; they are rather deep-seated dispositions (what Bourdieu, using a Latin word, calls a *habitus*) infused throughout a person's life, bringing into intelligible order diverse aspects of a person such as preferences for food, interpersonal norms of conduct, beliefs about appropriate subjects for photography and taste in music. As Blake remarked, in reviewing one of Bourdieu's major works:

> the psychological and bodily intimacy and scope of habitus suggests the scale of the odds stacked against certain kinds of educational endeavour. It illuminates the suspicion that 'Mozart for the masses', for instance, is a project hamstrung by far more than mere inverted snobbery, ignorance or the malign influence of the industries of popular culture. (1992, p. 273)

What can we say briefly to these suggestions? One elementary point is that the sort of sociology Bourdieu offers us definitely undermines any appeal to psychological obstacles. Taking Chomsky's obvious point that there are many things humans simply cannot do naturally (such as build nests), once they are asked to do things they *can* do, humans can achieve whatever is asked of them. This is the sort of point that is made when one notes that any baby can be brought up to learn any human language, however superficially different languages may be and however superficially different the babies may be. Bourdieu will no doubt draw our attention to the different things different groups of speakers and users of the same language do with it, to how they use it and its varieties to distinguish themselves in the ways we have just alluded to in cultural practices. But all this differentiating can only work if the people involved do share a common grasp of the language concerned.

The point then is that, as far as using things to distinguish themselves is concerned, there is really no limit on what can be used. At one time, groups may espouse ballet versus can-can, at another they might exploit differences between Russian traditions of dance and English ones. We may as a matter of fact find distinct constellations of aesthetic taste characterising dominant and dominated groups in a social formation, but nothing in the theory requires those distinctions; others would do as well. So there is scope for changes in the direction we desire.

Another more materialist (in a Marxist sense) aspect of Bourdieu's thought roots different aesthetic attitudes in economic relations. Disinterestedness and intellectual play require a certain degree of freedom from the exigencies of production for survival. No doubt they do. But here again things do not stand still. It is mildly encouraging, when one reads Arnold lamenting the deplorable condition of the working class in nineteenth-century England and notes possible parallels with the situation of the poor in our contemporary 'third world', to reflect on the substantial amelioration of the condition of at least a large proportion of Arnold's group over the intervening century. We are not suggesting that there is no need to worry about overpopulation and the carrying capacity of the earth, but we are suggesting that, for most groups, standards of living and the relative distance from the exigencies of production for survival have increased. It is possible, then, to hope that more and more people can reach a stage when they can afford (literally and metaphorically) the circumstances appropriate to the enjoyment of high culture.

A related point concerns formal schooling. People are apt to bemoan the cultural implications of universal schooling. One point to remember here is that very few societies have yet had much experience of universal schooling beyond the primary years. In England it has only been since the 1944 Act that all children are expected to receive a secondary education (and for most it stopped at 14 years of age anyway). In some of the English-speaking islands of the Caribbean many children still finish their schooling in All-Age schools which are simply primary schools with a couple more age-cohorts added on. Provision of secondary schooling has changed considerably within the short period we are considering. We are not therefore yet in a position to know either what universal secondary schooling has achieved nor, more obviously, what it might achieve.

INTELLIGENCE

A rather different but related conception of education and culture has been presented in recent work by R. S. Barrow. In his book *Language, Intelligence and Thought* (1993) he develops a model of education which he claims derives from a proper understanding of the notion of intelligence. Part of the interest of this is that here we have a modern attempt to appeal to psychology to underpin a narrow focus for education in very much the same way that Bantock does. Although Barrow says very little directly about culture he does see that his analysis is, and must be, culturally specific (1993, p. 84) and it is certainly the case that it bears upon the types of cultural transmission which we are concerned with in the present work. For Barrow, 'an intelligent person is one who can distinguish, recognise, and deal appropriately with dimensions to a question, claim or problem that are, variously, empirical, conceptual, aesthetic, moral, mathematical, historical, religious, and interpersonal' (1993, p. 83) which seems a fairly generous spread of achievements. He does not deny that there may be other ways of classifying understanding, such as the 'political or the sociological', but thinks that the types of awareness contained in the above list are more fundamental than these. So, for instance, the 'political' might be investigated conceptually, empirically or historically. However, for all the apparent generosity of this list, Barrow's particular arguments seem to support a conception of both education and intelligence that is less than generous.

Barrow insists, correctly, that there are conceptual relationships between intelligence, understanding and rationality but his spelling out of these relationships seems distinctly curious. So, for instance, he writes:

> unintelligent people are so called because they display a capacity to misunderstand, in the sense of get their thinking wrong. They fail to grasp arguments, to proceed logically, to take account of evidence that is brought to their attention, to recognise evidence as evidence. The intelligent person is one who is able to engage in rational argument in a way that observes the rules of sound reasoning. (1993, p. 56)

The argument here seems to move from the general—and probably sound—to the particular and distinctly dubious. And the doubt concerns the fact that Barrow seems to take one form of unintelligence, not being able to deal with arguments, as the paradigm of all forms of unintelligence. So, being intelligent is being able to argue well and being unintelligent is the reverse. That the linguistic and the logical (in the precise sense of the word) are the marks of intelligence are explicitly avowed by Barrow in the pages that follow. However, the intelligent person does not merely have to exhibit a grasp of argument in one domain (for instance they could, in Barrow's words, have a 'massive understanding' of physics and still be unintelligent) rather they have to exhibit this grasp across a range of humanly important areas. And some areas count more than others, so that environmental and gender issues may be handled by someone in a well-informed, erudite and sensible way but that person might still count as unintelligent (1993, p. 56).

This is very confusing and, we think, confused but to see why it is one has to go back to basics. As this partly turns upon definitions it is as well to start with these. Linguistic analysis of the type that Barrow is engaged in can serve two functions. First, it may be a clarification of the way we actually use words. Much, for instance, of the work of the later Wittgenstein, including his celebrated comments about games (see Wittgenstein, 1958), is an attempt to draw attention to the way in which we use language and the implications of such usage for our thought about the world. Second, and necessarily derivatively, analysis can go beyond actual usage—because such usage can be shown to be incoherent, muddled or vague—and amount to a recommendation to apply our concepts in a different way. Such a recommendation cannot, of course, be true or false—that is not the type of thing recommendations can be—but has to be considered as more or less useful. In this particular case Barrow must be engaged in the second type of exercise. And this is necessarily so because, as a matter of fact, most people do regard someone who has a 'massive understanding' of physics as intelligent. So if Barrow wants to claim that this is mistaken he is going beyond current usage.

Given that his analysis is a recommendation of this type, how do we assess its usefulness? If, as we have admitted above, intelligence is linked to understanding and rationality then, perhaps, via some clarification of these concepts. The problem here is that both of these concepts are equivocal and therefore care is needed in tracing their connections to intelligence. So, for instance, understanding can mean a wide and deep knowledge of a particular field, for instance, physics or history. But with this usage it cannot be equivalent to intelligence because we are quite happy, with good reason, to credit trainee physicists and historians with intelligence in these particular areas even although they cannot, as yet, claim wide or deep knowledge. On the other hand understanding may refer to procedure rather than content. (These two things are not totally distinct in either physics or history, that is, you cannot proceed in either without some grasp of content, but they are distinct enough to make our point.) So a novice may exhibit this kind of understanding if they show awareness of the type of enquiry they are engaged in, the problems they face and the ways in which such problems can and cannot be resolved. If Barrow's dismissal of the 'massive understanding' of the trained physicist is meant simply to draw attention to this alternative notion of understanding, then this is all to the good. However, it appears difficult to see it as just this. Because, if the tyro is intelligent because he is, to put it crudely, doing it right at this level then, presumably, the person with a 'massive understanding' will still be doing it right at hers and, of course, she will have the depth and breadth as well. So there is no reason to withhold the accolade of intelligence from her too.

Rationality and its connections to intelligence require similar caution. The intelligent must, in some way, be the rational. However, there are different ways of being rational. One important but narrow way is in obeying the canons of argument in the way in which Barrow mentions and so, for instance, realising that contradicting yourself is not a sound method of trying to conduct an argument. But rationality has its place in other activities apart from arguments. Famously—and there is a very large literature on this—it also has to do with fitting means to ends in purposive action. So, for example, if you want a given end, say, to win the Football Premiership, there will be ways of acting which are conducive to this end, such as training and thinking about the opposition teams, and ways of acting which are not, such as selling all your best players. This type of rationality, let us call it practical rationality, spreads far beyond the use of argument. Which is not to say that it cannot be, sometimes, captured in argument. We may talk about such things as well as do them. But the doing comes first. It is only because we can see that some things work in practice and others do not, that it becomes sensible to argue for one course of action rather than another. What sort of things can be done rationally in this sense of the word? A vast range of things from the level of making a bed to the level of running a country, which includes participation in areas such as physics and history. So, given an accepted range of ends, one can argue, engage in love affairs, build bridges, play football, do philosophy, play chess, run a meeting, and so on, more or less rationally. Change the end and you change the appropriate means so, if you just want to win the argument logically, following the canons of logic is a required means. If, however, the argument is with Pedro the Cruel and you want to stay healthy, it might be totally irrational to point out his contradictions.

Again, both understandings of rationality fit well with intelligence. We do think that people who display rationality of argument are manifesting their intelligence, but we also think such intelligence may be made manifest in engaging in the practicalities of life. The more complex the argument or the practicality, the more both will call for intelligence. The key here is to realise that at its basic level the notion of intelligence must be adverbial. That it must characterise a way—or better, ways—of doing things. For it is only by observing what people do that we can tell whether they—as people—are intelligent or not. But it would be very strange to think—as Barrow seems to—that only linguistic doings, that is, speech and writing, merit the title of intelligent because very often such doings are simply a report and assessment of non-linguistic doing. So, to intelligently assess Wellington as a military commander or Bobby Charlton as a footballer is, in these cases at least, to assess how intelligently Wellington commanded and Charlton played, and it would surely be odd to think that talking about something must—in the intelligence stakes— take precedence over doing it. (This fits in with the manifest fact that very often those who can do some things supremely well, for example 'read' a battle or a football game, are manifestly inadequate when it comes to talking about such things.)

So far, our analysis keeps hold of Barrow's insistence that intelligence is tied conceptually to the notions of understanding and rationality. However, unlike Barrow, our account both stays closer to accepted usage and, because this is so, it is much more accommodating to ideas of practical intelligence which may be transcribed into words but need not be. Are there any further reasons for either restricting or extending the above notions in the ways that Barrow seems to recommend?

Barrow gestures towards usefulness when he talks of understanding:

> If nothing is to be said of types of understanding, the concept is so broad as to be of little practical value, since everybody, in having some understanding would have a degree of intelligence, and nobody would come anywhere near the ideal, since nobody understands all there is to be understood. (1993, p. 54)

This is obviously right in some ways but, just as obviously, wrong in others. It is correct in that we do, with both intelligence and understanding, have to cash these terms in particular contexts. So, to be told that a person understands or is intelligent is to be told very little unless we are also told the type of thing that they are supposed to understand or the type of area in which they do display intelligence. However, the fact that these notions are often used elliptically, that is, without the context of their use being fully spelled out, does not make them 'of little practical value'. Rather, it is the fact that these are general terms which have to be cashed in particular contexts and which therefore, for cashing, have to invoke the standards of these contexts, which makes such terms enormously useful. Few people seem to think that terms such as 'equality' and 'need', which also lend themselves to elliptical usage, are therefore of no practical value. That we have to take care how we use such terms is one of the duties that the richness of our language imposes upon us.

As far as 'the ideal' is concerned, the question to ask here is 'whose ideal?' No sensible person could have, as a remotely realistic ideal, a conception of either understanding or intelligence which was supposed to encompass everything. Such an ideal would be useless, and it would be so because it would offend against one of the manifest facts of human nature: that the performances of human beings tend to vary in excellence depending upon context—that somebody, say, who displays intelligence or understanding within the realms of philosophy or physics, may display neither when it comes to football or films; that the person who is masterful at literary criticism is simply stupid in conducting their love life. Barrow attempts to cut through the facts of human variability with the notion of 'fundamental importance'. So, for instance, he writes:

> It is, in other words, part of the meaning of the word that people who are intelligent should have broad understanding and understanding of whatever can be shown to be of fundamental importance. (1993, p. 57)

But this is an attempt to avoid the ellipses brought about by such variability by yet another elliptical usage. Any mention of 'fundamental importance' invites the questions: 'for whom?' and 'for what?' And, as soon as such questions are asked, it becomes clear that what is of fundamental importance in one context is irrelevant in others.

So, for instance, if you are lost in the Kalahari desert an intelligent guide—rather than, say, an intelligent literary critic—may be of fundamental importance. When trying to score a goal in football a person's understanding of history may simply be irrelevant. What counts in running a country may not count in running a love affair. We may, of course, if we wish, follow Barrow's recommendation that we only award the accolade of 'understanding' and 'intelligence' to those who exhibit such traits in more than one context. And it is true that we regard those who excel at only one thing as unduly narrow. But we should not, as Barrow seems to do, believe that, in going beyond the particular, we have found another and different use of 'understanding' and 'intelligence'. All usage of these terms, in the end, has to be cashed in particular contexts and to insist that only some combinations of these contexts count is simply to misunderstand this basic fact, and to nail your colours to the mast of yet another, highly artificial and highly disputable, particular context. So, for example, if $x_1 \ldots x_n$ are all the possible areas of human excellence—in terms of understanding and intelligence—any claim that only $x_1 + x_5 + x_8$ really count, is bound to be met with, at least two objections. First, why do we need this stipulation at all? Second, given this particular stipulation, why should we not allow counter-stipulation, say, $x_3 + x_7 + x_{13}$ or $x_1 + x_{10} + x_{19}$? Given the facts of human nature and the fact, despite Barrow's seeming belief to the contrary, that we are often interested—both personally and professionally—with people's intelligence within physics, or politics, or management, as well as within and across, say, mathematics, literature and history, we are likely to come across both people whose performance in one area strikes us as excellent but who perform badly in others and also people whose combination of talents may be striking, but rather odd.

In the context of education, the suggestions of both Barrow and Bantock face other problems. If we privilege—and, in the light of the above, unreasonably privilege—one form of understanding and intelligence above all others, or we decide that only certain favoured contributions count, then our education system runs the risk of ignoring the capacities for excellence that people actually have and thus of treating some people unjustly. Any decent education system must be concerned about learning outcomes and must be concerned with equity. Any system that ignores or does not fully address the worthwhile talents of its pupils will offend against both of these concerns. A system based upon the predilections of either Bantock or Barrow will—and does—so offend.

6

The Plurality of Cultures

Arnold wrote in an educational tradition that both lay in a main line of descent from the cultural formations he most valued and equipped him with the tools necessary to appreciate many of the elements in those traditions that are not in his native language. So when he referred, as exemplars of high culture, to Homer and Cicero, Montesquieu and Goethe, he presumed acquaintance with their works in the original languages on his own part and on that of his audience. His own vernacular derived from that of Shakespeare and the Authorised Version of the Bible.

We have explicitly assumed a broader range for those things that our Arnoldian filter will identify, but this in itself is not particularly problematic. Restricting ourselves to the literary field (the other arts and cultural achievements present analogies), we can make two obvious points. There is more than enough excellence available in a sub-set of the languages and literature that might be educationally salient to be going on with. Ezra Pound may have found an unsurpassed musicality in Old Provençal, but it remains true that people can appreciate the sound of poetry well enough from examples in Greek, Italian, English and no doubt in Japanese as well.

That brings us to the second obvious comment, that cultures with comprehensive achievements can be regarded educationally as virtually self-sufficient. When Bertrand Russell (1968, Vol. II, p. 126) remarked that an educated Chinaman was the most civilised type of person to be found, he did not assume that this Chinaman had also acquired a nodding acquaintance with Homer and Shakespeare—the culture of China was sufficient in itself.[1]

OUTSIDERS

So someone like Arnold addressing an audience similarly placed, or even supposed as addressing an audience in an analogous place in a different comprehensively achieved culture, begins with a crucial advantage over the rest of us. They are on the inside; the rest of the world is outside. They speak one at least of the languages in which things are conducted. The dimensions of possible exclusion here include class, gender, and ethnicity. Arnold was preoccupied with the need for state-supported secondary schooling for the middle class, and we have seen that he did not in the end regard high culture as necessarily élitist, the preserve of a minority of a society. But sadly the fact too often is that much conspires to give the best that has been said and done a class colouring: it becomes a badge of particular sub-groups, a crucial element of 'cultural capital' and not the common currency of an entire group.

So too we can and do find gender differences in access to and involvement in these things, and deeply rooted stereotyping that helps to perpetuate them. None of this seems necessarily the case; educationally it presents us with a challenge to overcome rather than an objection in principle to our undertaking.

Ethnicity presents a harder nut to crack. Leaving aside a mythical globalisation that will erase all cultural and ethnic differences as an unlikely fantasy, we are faced with the fact that many people are cut off from the cultural traditions we have invoked both by language and by histories of repression and domination that give them, even when accessible in some form, a negative charge that makes commitment ambivalent and encourages the discovery or invention of alternatives. How can you embrace a culture which usually stereotypes you as a worthless sub-human? Why ever should anyone want to?

Language alone is a relatively minor problem. It is perhaps difficult for English-speakers, with the grossly inadequate teaching of foreign languages that they typically receive and the low level of motivation for acquiring them that the global position of English now gives them, to appreciate how common it is for people to be bi- or multi-lingual. From an educational point of view it is important to distinguish cases where all a person's languages are written and the educationally more difficult case where a person's mother tongue is as yet unwritten.[2] But in general the fact that there is nothing much to read in one's own language does not necessarily prevent most speakers of it from acquiring a language in which there is enough to read. And there is also the simple point that translation is possible, though there are practical difficulties offsetting this fact: a language with a small number of speakers may not find translators of sufficient quality to convey more than the literal gist of texts in other languages; it may not provide a profitable market for publication; and when it is unwritten, translation will be ephemeral, unless, as often happens, the occasion of translation is also the motivation for developing a written form of the language.

Even if we can argue away the importance of purely linguistic barriers, the fact remains that cultures are often alien to each other and often hostile. Many learners are either not within a high cultural tradition at all or are there as dominated colonials, a position evocatively presented in much Caribbean autobiographical writing, for instance.

High culture is learned; for no one does it come naturally. But there are clearly crucial differences between Naipaul or C. L. R. James in Trinidad, working-class children in Birmingham, and the children of Bernstein's 'new' middle class whose status derives from intimate traffic in cultural goods. For the last two groups, there is a degree of common knowledge and acceptance of the relevant high culture that was not to be found in early twentieth-century Trinidad. Of course, Trinidad is not and was not homogeneous. But we can agree that it was relevantly further removed than almost anything in the contemporary British Isles.

Attending to the broadly aesthetic or humanistic aspects of high culture, we can argue that even for people so divorced from a tradition, and indeed for anyone else, initiation into it does not entail simple acceptance of values that are proffered in its canonical texts.[3] It is obvious that much that is excellent in important respects is unacceptable in others—literary studies have long worried at the suspension of disbelief involved when we appreciate the merits of a work of art that seems to express an absurd or immoral outlook. Asking people to read Aeschylus is not to ask them to condone sacrificing one's daughter to get the fleet under way. To appreciate Dante one does not have to accept his (or any) theology. That Aristotle and Hume have obnoxious views on slavery or Africans does not undermine their place in the history of philosophy, though it cautions us against uncritical discipleship.[4]

It may be said that it is easy for us to separate the Hume who made the justification of induction a central issue in philosophy from the Hume who casually made obnoxious remarks about Negroes in Jamaica, but it is not so easy for a typical Jamaican to make this separation. It may be true that Hume does not make disparaging remarks about ordinary Englishmen, but even if he did this would not be the point. We could brush any such remark off; we have a confidence born of belonging that is not shared so easily by those who are made painfully aware that they do not belong and are not welcomed by many of those who do. As Mills has said:

> one is thrust into a world in which official theory proclaims one's inferiority, one's diminished person...The European agent can move confidently about this world, because in large measure it is a world he has created. He looks into the Universe and his own face looks approvingly back; he is getting recognition signals wherever he goes, but when a non-European looks, he finds the reflection of another's face. (1997, p. 63)

MORE CHOICES

The distortion and oppression are real enough. We hesitate to make a case that may seem to underplay their significance, but we want to

suggest that we have here ultimately the same kind of issue we have
noticed with respect to class and gender. Of the myriad things that are
true of a person, which are salient for him or her? How do they
characterise themselves? And we want to claim that these questions of
self-conception are more matters for voluntary choice than unalter-
able fact, that what is important, what tradition one selects to
espouse, are better regarded as choices, matters that can be given
more or less salience, or where different selections are possible, than
as given by birth or the events of one's life. With these claims we have
moved largely out of the aesthetic side of high culture into central
issues for the other aspect of Arnold's concern: the criticism of stock
notions, the Socratic search for a reflectively sustainable life.[5]

In considering which predicates are salient for a person it is
important to remember that we cannot pretend that each person can
choose for themselves. It must be acknowledged that, whatever their
personal preferences, what other people around them think is salient
becomes so. Of course, for many features people cannot, or can
hardly, choose to change anyway. One's age is fixed, and one's gender
almost as much. So is the chemical composition of one's liver, but this
is not something people are likely to be concerned with. A feature is
worth being concerned about if it makes a difference in some area
that one is independently concerned about. If being female affects an
important capacity differently from being male, then there is a reason
to be concerned about gender in that context. As Plato recognised, if
gender makes no difference it ought not to be made to play a part in
maintaining differences.

But it is also important to recognise that there are few necessities
here—it is salient that we are material beings, animals for whom
air, water, food are essential, whether or not we wish to dwell on
these things. We may even despise them, but we cannot live
without them (cf. Graham, 1996). But it is not necessarily salient
that we have skin of this colour or that, that we descend from a
Serbian Orthodox family or a Bosnian Muslim one. These things
become salient thanks to people's choices and activity. People who
wish to insist on their importance will often insist on their
essentiality, but falsely. The tragic problem for so many is that
when people have made them salient it is often virtually impossible,
in the short run, to undermine this salience and replace it with
other contrasts upon which to construct social and political life.

The political goal of education and other activity should, we think,
be to allow people to exercise as much freedom here as is possible, so
that they are not tied to socially given scripts (Appiah's expression in
his contribution to Gutmann, 1994), but are empowered to pick and
choose their own 'identity' as they wish. What our Arnoldian
approach offers them is the chance to rummage among the best

options there have been in so constructing what matters to them (which is not only a present 'identity' but a tradition or set of traditions too, as well as exemplars, standards, heroes and heroines).

Culturally, and we would say also politically, the ideal being offered is a form of cosmopolitanism. This was implicit in Arnold's position. And not merely the cosmopolitanism of a person firmly set in one cultural tradition but open to the accomplishments of others— the sort of weak multiculturalism Scruton (1998) finds in Mahler's setting of German translations of Chinese poetry. What Arnold describes and celebrates is rather the miscegenation of cultural traditions, what in some contexts is discussed as creolisation, the mixing of cultural traditions and creation of something distinctively different as a result. This was in effect what he described and advocated in his account of modern Western civilisation as a confluence of Hebraism and Hellenism, and what he praised in his insalubrious remarks about the English mixture of Celtic, German and Norman 'bloods' (Trilling, 1939, p. 240, and see pp. 232–243 for some judicious remarks on Arnold's invocation of race). The possibility of creolisation goes some way to disarming Anderson's criticism of Arnold that Hebraism and Hellenism are not comple- mentary but conflicting forces (Anderson, 1962). Conquerors and conquered can mix, both physically and culturally.

Nussbaum has recently been prominent in advocating cosmo- politanism and world citizenship[6] as ideals for our education and politics. One may distinguish various positions here. At one extreme, world political unity has been urged, as by L. J. Cohen (1954), but these days it has few defenders. We suspect this is mainly a matter of empirical observation—the chances of the world getting Scandina- vian good sense rather than brutal dictatorship or unedifying asset- stripping are not worth gambling on—since it does seem to be the obvious direction for moral thought. Local, contingent relationships have proved less amenable to moral thinking, at least since Plato abolished the family in his utopia (see Winfield, 1998, pp. 132–136, for criticism of families on the grounds of, *inter alia*, partiality). Even if local attachments to family, friends, colleagues and so on can find a place in a defensible moral theory, there does not seem to be anything to underwrite the enormous chasms that national boundaries *de facto* create among people.[7] Efficiencies of feasible scale may well make mega-groupings too large for collective action, though it is not clear we have any evidence to support this notion. But even if they do, they do not generate the vast differences among feasible collectivities that we actually find among nations. The cosmopolitanism we urge is intended to shatter 'the way the national imagination even of progressives remains in thrall to [their national] borders, routinely unwilling or unable to register the moral and political weight of non-citizens' as Robbins has recently noted (1998, p. 13).

But if we simply compromise with currently overwhelming social forces and admit as brute contingencies the actual nation states we happen to find, we can, as Nussbaum insists, rank our loyalties to these (and it is worth noting that individual persons may have ties of nationality to more than one nation—one of the authors has a child who is eligible for three nationalities) in such a way as to give our fundamental loyalty to '*no* mere form of government, no temporal power, but to the moral community made up by the humanity of all human beings' (Nussbaum, 1997, p. 59) or to some ideal federation of nations of a kind advocated by Kant.[8] And as Cicero (in *De Officiis*, for instance)[9] or Appiah (1998) have argued one can value patriotism or what John White has dubbed 'national sentiment' (1996) more highly and yet retain a cosmopolitan concern. As Plamenatz remarked some time ago, the crucial distinction is with nationalism: 'patriotism is a love of one's people which does not carry with it hostility to strangers, whereas nationalism is emotionally in arms against the foreigner, the intruder, the outsider' (1960, p. 13).

All the same, we have to recognise the tremendous pressures that now support nationalist projects of a kind that do not sit easily with our preferred cosmopolitanism. As Gellner put it:

> Nationalism did not invent identity, any more than it invented the wheel. Yet identity *is* relevant to nationalism. Nationalism has profoundly changed *the nature of that with which men identify*. Previously they identified, roughly, with their location in a social hierarchy, in a structure of positions. The fact that their 'culture' (style of speech, dress, consumption, etc.) was not the same as that of occupants of other near-by positions, did not undermine a person's confidence in the continued occupancy of his own niche: on the contrary, it reinforced it. Cultural differences sustained political cohesion, rather than putting it under stress. They were markers which helped identify the position and differentiate it from its neighbours: they greatly helped him to slot himself into the right place, and to stop others usurping that place. Now, suddenly, men live in a musical-chairs world in which they only occupy locations very briefly, without firm or deep commitment, but what does matter to them is their mastery of and acceptability in a culture, which delimits the range of positions within which they may settle without discomfort and objection. It is this which engenders nationalism (pre-occupation with culture-membership and the political protection of the culture and the collectivity it defines). Nationalism heralds, not the coming or re-affirmation of identity, but a novel and peculiar form of it, incompatible with old political forms and engendering new ones. (1996, p. 629)

The social forces Gellner identified behind the rise of nationalism make it imperative, in our view, for responsible education to aim determinedly towards a more comprehensive viewpoint. It is another case of the objection to including too much of the familiar in the curriculum—people are going to get their national or ethnic identity rammed home by any number of agencies and pressures; let the school fight for something else.

Cosmopolitanism as we see it seeks the best wherever it may be found. It is not in the business of withholding judgement across cultures, rather the reverse. In the realm of art it eagerly seeks out the best, and attempts to grasp genres and approaches that are distinctive—the role of calligraphy in Chinese art, for instance, or the tea ceremony. In less exalted circles it wants to learn by comparison what are the effects of different social policies and of different cultural practices (in a wide sense). We can borrow Nerlich's view of a culture as 'an engineering programme for producing persons' (1989, p. 17), permitting and preferably calling forth human flourishing.[10] As he says:

> whether a culture does all this is no more a matter of subjective feeling or opinion than whether a fitness programme leads to stronger, more flexible, or more agile bodies. Whatever we like to think, capitalist cultures tend to corrupt social relationships, for example. (1989, p. 18)

Since controlled experiments are rarely possible here we may not always be able to get completely unambiguous results, but surely we can do so often enough to determine the intellect either to give or to withhold its consent, in Mill's words, about the effects of easy access to guns, of the prohibition of alcohol and other recreational drugs, of the nugatory deterrent consequences of death penalties, and of much more. Nerlich's own preferred comparisons, of cultures' scope for promoting what he regards as distinctive in our moral life, may well be more difficult to make, but, as we have seen, he thinks they are not impossible. He offers reasons for thinking that Aztecs and Nazis, at least, suffered from cultures that had gone badly wrong in these respects (1989, pp. 193–194).

The form of cosmopolitanism we advocate offers respect, initially, to cultures as attempts to provide a way of life, just as our moral stance would offer respect to other persons as autonomous agents. But in neither case is there is any reason not to notice rampant injustice, exploitation, lying, coercion or the denial of a voice to enormous numbers of people. As Hamlet says, 'use every man after his desert and who would 'scape whipping?' Cultures have not made much progress in providing universal justice, self-respect, and most other fundamental goods that have been suggested. So Taylor's proposal (in Gutmann, 1994) that actual cultures be accorded equal respect is, as he recognises, more than dubious if understood as commending them equally, or as supposing that their artistic and other products are of equal value. Recalling the discussion in Chapter

1, we could add that cultures do not in general have a good record for promoting critical thought.

LIBERALISM, PLURALISM, AND EDUCATION

Since we are working from an educational perspective it may be worth noting that the typical educational context, the initiation of the young into a tradition, gives a special twist to some of the political issues relating to cultural differences. At least, it does when education is conceived, as Arnold did, as critical rather than simply as socialisation.

A crude characterisation of the liberal spirit might be 'live, and let live'. Simple differences in practice are generally unproblematic. You may not eat frogs' legs or snails or sweet-potato leaves, but no great harm is done to your well-being by letting other people do so. It is where such practices enter what we take to be the moral sphere that toleration becomes problematic. But even here we may need to draw lines between what we regard as immoral but legally tolerable and what we regard as simply intolerable. Suttee does not comport well with most views or laws about homicide; nor female circumcision with those on assault and bodily harm.

Galston (1989, p. 100) reminds us that it would be illiberal to insist on everyone following Socratic injunctions to examine and reflect on what is valuable. Liberals must let people live unexamined lives. Their concern arises only when such people try to stop others getting on with their own preferred lifestyle. If liberals should let people get on with their lives, always excepting infringements on the equal liberty of others, it might seem that liberals should let people get on with bringing up their children pretty much how they like. Unexamined modes of life can be reproduced. Let people get on with it.

From such a perspective, a multicultural context creates practical problems for organised school systems and taxpayers, but hardly a problem of principle. Consenting adults reproduce their social relations minute by minute. If that is acceptable, so presumably is the activity they undertake to initiate newcomers into such social relations.

That way of putting it is intended to suggest two serious doubts about this line of thought. The first is whether all the people indeed so consent; we shall leave this aside for the moment. The second is more directly relevant to education, and is the simple fact that the people involved are typically not adult. Liberalism takes people as adults, as they are, and does not inquire how they came to be that way. It respects and attributes responsibility to them. It does not confront them with counterfactual possibilities: if you were to reflect on things, you might prefer something else, or (closer perhaps to educational concerns, though yet more difficult to substantiate) if you had attended to those issues at school, you would now prefer something else. Now, however appropriate it may be to treat adults as adults, it is not at all clear that we can get away with treating children similarly. What it is acceptable for adults to do with adults may not be acceptable for adults to do with the young. If a child were properly thought of as an adult's property, then possibly a liberal's concern would only extend to the constraints on what those adults might do. But however much a child may be assigned to one or more adults as the person or persons 'responsible for' him or her, we must recognise some perhaps expanding centre of interests that the child has or is intrinsically, which themselves put constraints on what the rest of us may properly do. It is not just that a child will most likely survive to become at some future time another adult, but rather that the child already has in some form or other the distinguishing marks of responsible personhood (see Brandon, 1995, for some brief remarks on the logical complexity we can expect in this context). The difficulty for theoretical liberalism is to find grounds to permit any interference with a child's own inclinations rather than to circumscribe parental authority (cf. Brandon, 1979; Harris, 1982), although this latter is by far the more pressing practical problem.

It is a truism that the educational literature is replete with conceptions of education that tell us that in this context of bringing children into the human fold we have some special obligations to them that we do not have towards adults. As we have stressed in discussing conceptions of culture, there is a consensus that what schools offer is coloured by normative conceptions. But the important point is that within this range of conceptions of education there are some, like Arnold's, which stress intellectual detachment from the socially given, and promote intellectual independence and autonomy. Far from being seamlessly part of everyday life, education, on such views, is a matter of doing different things, of being exposed to different things, of expanding horizons, and of promoting critical reflection on these possibilities.

While education conceived of as critique cannot require that those exposed to it eventually endorse the critical spirit (relapsing into the unexamined life must remain a possibility), such an approach to education can hardly be seen as merely social reproduction. As John Anderson (for instance, 1962) recognised, to the extent that it impinges on learners, it is instead subversive of many modes of social life. It is likely to cut people somewhat adrift from their social moorings.[11] Nor is it a particularly congenial site for toleration.[12] We want learners to get things right, not just do any old thing that occurs to them or is customary in their social milieu, as we noted at the end of Chapter 1. Educationally the difficulty arises, not in general from practices taken in themselves (such as running in the corridor or wearing particular clothes, which schools often disallow for various good or bad reasons), but from such practices taken with their associated beliefs. If someone thinks that cooked sweet-potato leaves are harmful, he or she is simply mistaken, and an Arnoldian conception of education strongly suggests that, other things being equal, we ought not to let someone remain thus mistaken. It is indeed this element in the conception that leads liberals to believe that political tolerance of misguided creeds such as Nazism permits reason to triumph over ignorance, since free debate, freely entered into, should lead people to acknowledge the errors built into their prejudices.

Of course, the difficulty is compounded by the fact that typically practice does come with associated beliefs and the mixture may be extremely complex. You do not just burn a widow the way you may choose whether to eat callaloo. What we find is usually a complex mixture of what some of us wish still to distinguish as facts and values.[13] The mixture may not be inextricable in principle, but its complexity is such that in practice we may not be able to make much headway. How to characterise the components of a view that makes the value of a widow's life less than her immolation?

So far it would seem that we have a choice for a liberal. Choose education as reproduction and endorse the varied and often illiberal practices of pluralist societies; choose education as critical reflection and face hostility from many groups whose way of life seems threatened by critical reflection or exposure to alternatives.

We may remark here in passing that notable liberal theorists can be found making both types of choice, though perhaps with little direct help from their theoretical positions. Nagel, at one point, endorses what sounds like our preferred conception—a 'maximal' approach to educational provision:

> The tendency toward equality and distrust of the exceptional found in the public educational systems of some modern liberal societies is a great mistake. Equality of opportunity is fine, but if a school system also tries to iron out distinctions, the waste from failure to exploit talent to the fullest is inexcusable... A society should try to foster the creation and preservation of what is best, or as good as it possibly can be, and this is just as important as the widespread dissemination of what is merely good enough. (1991, p. 135)

On the other hand, Rawls takes education as an example of the difference between the consequences of a comprehensive liberalism, which promotes autonomy and individuality, and his own political liberalism, which:

> requires far less. It will ask that children's education include such things as knowledge of their constitutional and civic rights so that, for example, they

know that liberty of conscience exists in their society and that apostasy is not a legal crime, all this to insure that their continued membership when they come of age is not based simply on ignorance of their basic rights or fear of punishment for offenses that do not exist. Moreover, their education should also prepare them to be fully cooperating members of society and enable them to be self-supporting; it should also encourage the political virtues so that they want to honor the fair terms of social cooperation in their relations with the rest of society. (1993, pp. 199–200)

It is a consequence of this position that Rawls would accept a far more minimal common educational system than that advocated by Nagel. One hesitates to comment briefly on Rawls, but a question does seem to arise of the units of political liberalism: is each individual to sign up to the contract, presumably understanding its bases, or will some simply be spoken for by their guardians, heads of household, or whatever? If each individual is to grasp the rationale for political liberalism, one may reasonably doubt Rawls' denial, omitted from the quotation above, that minimal political education need not confront the issues endorsed by a comprehensive liberalism.[14]

To return to the main argument, illiberal groups of consenting adults can only maintain a liberal polity by accident. If liberalism is to be non-accidentally sustained, some people at least must come to endorse it. As Gutmann (1987) has done for democracy, we can then try to motivate one of the educational choices rather than the other by reference to what is necessary for the continuing reproduction among new members of a liberal polity. And that is pretty clearly the critical conception; it is only reproduction in the special case where the social group is already thoroughly liberal in its views.[15]

To connect the discussion again with Rawls, there is a distinction between what has to be done to defend liberal society against illiberal groups within it (where expediency may well suggest an unwilling tolerance of undesirable practices that would, ideally, be proscribed) and the minimal requirements for allowing liberal or non-liberal groups that do not endorse individualistic values to live together across generations. One could be forgiven for seeing his overriding concern to preserve peace among probably unwilling neighbours as in effect giving up on the conditions necessary for those neighbours' children to receive an adequate grounding in the principles that guide the larger polity.

Another route to the same educational conclusion is provided by considerations Nagel (1987) once used to articulate liberalism's way of identifying conflicts. He contended that it was recognition of the lack of common ground for resolution of differences of opinion that distinguishes those cases where liberalism insists on tolerance. In some cases opposing sides do share common ground and a non-question begging explanation is available for their differences. So believers in cold fusion operate on the same assumptions as other physicists; one day, their errors (if they are wrong) will be understood in terms of experimental errors or miscalculations or whatever. But in other contexts there is no common ground, nor a mutually acceptable explanation of what eventually turns out to be error. People occupying different positions with regard to, say, religion may not wish to acknowledge the epistemological situation they find themselves in, but it just is a fact that the differences here are not differences within a common framework but differences about the framework itself. Where there is common ground, Nagel says we can make decisions that endorse one view from among its competitors, but where there is not, we must refrain from doing so since that would be to impose a view that its opponents cannot see as justifiable.[16] (Nagel suggested that we should not appeal to truth in politics, but this view appeals at least to second order meta-truths about the presence or absence of agreement, which on his view are surely a kind of truth.)

Now a curriculum designed to sustain liberalism is going to have to look at the contrast between decidable and undecidable issues, and at the epistemological status of items on both sides of the divide. But again it is clear that a sober assessment of the epistemological status of religious, economic, cultural and other beliefs is a feature of the kind of education we have allocated to the critical side. Let us ask what would be the appropriate curriculum for dealing with these no-common ground issues: a curriculum which was epistemologically serious but neutral about the alternatives on offer. If students learn what they are told, it might seem that it would seriously undermine the systems of beliefs in question, since the message would be: there are fifty-seven varieties on offer and no reason to prefer one to another. And that is not far from saying 'a plague on all your houses'. This type of teaching is not the sort of thing promoted by closed societies, as for instance the parents in the Mozart[17] case saw. (They objected to school textbooks that treated different religions in an even-handed way.)

Nagel has changed the basis of his views on tolerance, and refers us to a paper by Raz (1990) in partial explanation. We are not sure what Nagel now thinks is wrong with his earlier position (it is not, we think, the point about meta-truths being truths). He still spends some time on epistemological issues—maintaining that there is a substantial middle ground between what it is unreasonable to believe and what it is unreasonable not to believe; that one may reasonably believe something while admitting that others may equally reasonably not accept it, despite shared evidence and reasoning. Rawls too seeks to limit public reason to principles 'independent of the opposing and conflicting philosophical and religious doctrines that citizens affirm' (1993, p. 9) and says that:

> a shared basis of justification that applies to comprehensive doctrines is lacking in the public culture of a democratic society. But such a basis is needed to mark the difference, in ways acceptable to a reasonable public, between comprehensive beliefs as such and true comprehensive beliefs. (p. 61)

Nagel wants everyone to be able to say, in some cases, 'I accept P (Christianity, say) but I think you are not unreasonable not to accept it', but in others 'I accept Q (the germ theory of disease, say [cf. Nagel, 1991, p. 161]) and I think you are unreasonable not to accept it'. As we understand Raz's objection to Nagel's earlier stance, the difficulty is to spell out a coherent sense in which you are reasonable to withhold assent while I am reasonable to accept a belief, when we are both confronted by the same reasons and evidence. Surely the only *reasonable* thing to do is to withhold assent until something good enough to determine acceptance (or rejection) becomes available for both of us.[18] But while that may be true when playing by the logic of ordinary everyday belief, the problem with moral, religious and ideological views in general is that we typically do not play by those rules, as Gellner claimed in discussing ideology. Politeness, if nothing else, encourages us to assume mutual reasonableness in these matters, but it is arguable that what we typically have is a wilful refusal to take a comprehensive view—we tinker with inherited beliefs at a few edges but do not in general ask whether the whole lot has anything going for it. But as Nagel notes (1991, p. 157), it is not only self-defeating to defend tolerance by arguing for the falsity of religious or other views that might reject it, it fails to capture an important element in the liberal defence: we tolerate for reasons you can endorse too, not for reasons you have to reject.

For this, perhaps Rawls' characterisation is sufficient. Members of different religions might be able to agree that a shared basis for adjudication among them does not exist, while it does for, say, questions about the aetiology of many diseases. Do they need to move from this recognition of difference to any normative *epistemological* judgement of reasonableness? As Ingram (1996, p. 157) suggests, there are other normative judgements they could use to bridge the gap to tolerance—a notion of moral integrity perhaps or of the significance of reason for morality—though she perhaps too easily supposes that we can pick out and exclude doctrines that are 'mad, irrational, or simply blind to everyday needs and interests' (1996, p. 154).[19]

We have tried to undermine a benign multicultural tolerance in the educational context by exploiting the difference between 'consenting adults' and the children we send to school. Adults can be left with their misrecognitions, to use Bourdieu's term; children must be offered weapons against cultural domination. But if misrecognition is deplorable in one case, surely it is in the other. Gutmann (1987) has asked how a democratic community can avoid imposing life-long education on its citizens; to take up an issue raised at the end of our first chapter, one may wonder how the position sketched above can avoid attacking the false assumptions of the adults, as well as alerting the children. Liberalism plus education for critical rationalism would then emerge as a universal enemy of cultural particularism, rather than a framework within which different groups might find space enough to survive.

CULTURAL CHANGE

As we have seen, the approach sketched above comes abruptly into conflict with views that suppose a cultural group has a right to perpetuate itself over generations. Many groups are hostile to changes of various sorts but our approach would often provide their young with access to such changes and an encouragement to experiment. So be it. We need not regret that no one now invokes Zeus or speaks Etruscan—except from the perspective of scholarship that would like to know more about how these things worked. If people now do not wish to continue speaking French in Quebec or Welsh in Wales (to use one of Arnold's own examples) we ought not to make them. Cultures change; if a change is likely from a morally acceptable occurrence, why prevent it?[20]

One response here might appeal to a substantial reading of the value of free speech: Skillen once asked us to 'suppose everybody walked out of the room every time unpopular views began to be expressed' (1982, p. 154). Audiences are essential for communication but, as Skillen emphasises also, free speech is sought in a society of equally voluntary persons. There would be little value in free speech if one's audience were in chains. We do not deny that it must be desolating to be the last generation speaking a language, with one's children communicating in some other tongue. But for all that, we deny that anyone has the right to insist on his or her child maintaining their mother tongue. As Taylor remarks, groups such as the Québecois wish to ensure future generations do as they do. But none of us has the right to insist on that. We speak only for ourselves; we do not speak for others, our spouses, children, servants or future descendants. Other people, including those in these categories, feature in our responsible moral and political thinking, but while liberalism asks us to think about other people it does not applaud our thinking for them, except in those exceptional cases when they clearly cannot think for themselves.[21] This seems to us the crucial individualist commitment of liberalism and what brings it into collision with any view in which one group of people are spoken for by another.

This fundamental individualism explains why there is a problem in a position Mendus has persuasively advocated, that we may 'come to see that as autonomy-valuers we lack the moral language with which to provide an explanation of their [Amish] humility as anything other than oppression' (1995, p. 200). We can indeed learn, as she says, that our moral perspective does not make room for the ways other societies have conceived themselves; we can let this insight temper our own self-confidence; but we cannot finally endorse these other perspectives without in a way committing moral suicide. One can of course choose to abandon thinking for oneself, one can become a disciple or lose oneself in an extremely anti-individualist society, but the banal point is that one cannot do these things and remain a liberal.

Bringing children up is a matter of perpetuating, reproducing, a culture. Educating them is a matter of exposing them to a wider range (in our terms, the best there is) with the consequent possibility that they will reject their starting point. It is one thing to let you live your way; it is another to let you try to ensure that your children grow up that way. It is tempting to construe liberalism in as procedural a way as possible (so that it makes the fewest substantive and presumably contentious commitments), and also to see it as provoking confrontation between ways of life in a dialogic search for human flourishing. But then the demands of Muslims for separate non-secular schools, or of the Amish for non-participation in state schooling, are opposed to the continuation of such dialogue. They want their children not to hear. It is true that liberalism must allow people to choose the unexamined life, but that is a consequence of liberalism in the political context, between consenting adults. When we focus on education as more than ground-level cultural reproduc-tion, it is far less clear that we should let sleeping minds lie.

It will be objected here that liberalism as pure procedure is not and cannot be a way of life. And pure procedure is itself impossible—procedures of social life must be expressed in a language (or in two or three, but not in all), must have a calendar, and much more culturally loaded baggage. Walzer (in Gutmann, 1994) has suggested that procedural liberalism is appropriate for a country such as the USA which sees itself as a nation of nations, but that other societies might find a liberalism that commits itself to the perpetuation of particular cultures more congenial. Of course the point still holds that the USA has to choose a language, or languages, to conduct its business, and thus cannot commit merely to procedures without any substantive cultural admixture. Groups may well be of one mind about a whole range of cultural activities and so find their policies perpetuating them. But once alternatives appear, policies that favour one culture over another should be seen for what they are. It seems to us that liberals concerned also that education, sweetness and light should prevail, should then be on guard against policies that restrict or obstruct people's liberty to adopt for themselves whatever cultural practices they may wish. On such a view, a child is harmed by being kept from dialogue that might change his or her life. If this means that in a few years the USA adopts Spanish as one of its official languages, so be it.

EDUCATION FOR CRITICAL CONSCIOUSNESS

What then might a critical educational liberalism look like? It has to acknowledge a starting point that is not itself part of liberalism—the substantive culture that pre-exists the procedure. But once that is granted, it aspires to the greatest proceduralism possible. Some substantive cultures can accommodate themselves to such a system, some cannot. The latter are directly challenged by a tolerant liberalism, since they cannot incorporate the tolerance. We can appeal to Nagel's factual claim to support the demand that, even so, tolerance should be adhered to. But this is to undermine those cultures. (Of course, cultures change through time and no doubt the liberal melting pot will yield a tolerant version of militant Islam at some future point—our claim is that that culture as it is now is incompatible with liberalism.) Its tolerance, its refraining from making decisions of certain sorts, is bound up with a sociological-cum-epistemological account of our predicament, and thus it gives centrality in its own self-understanding to these sorts of epistemo-logical questions, and thus to the consequences that may follow from attention to them.

Would all this—in a more rational world—lead to convergence? Perhaps so. And perhaps that is an objection to it, a vestige of a Platonic desire for uniformity and stasis. But is the thought of a significantly more rational world an appropriate move in this argument? It is pointless to inquire what perfectly rational beings would do when people as we know them are far from perfectly rational. We may compare Walzer's speculation about a future in which female autonomy and gender equality have triumphed:

> gender equality will take different forms in different times and places, and even in the same time and place among different groups of people, and some of these forms will turn out to be consistent with cultural difference. It may even happen that men will play a larger role in sustaining and reproducing the cultures they claim to value. (1997, p. 66)

We have the capacity for more individual and collective rationality than we currently display, but the forces massed against even a minuscule move in that direction are such that our position already has more than enough practical difficulties to overcome.

NOTES

1. We assume here that the identification and delimitation of these cultural traditions has already been made. We have emphasised earlier (in Chapter 2) that decisions here are often pretty arbitrary.
2. Arguably this is the situation of many children in the Caribbean and elsewhere for whom literacy is inextricably tied up with mastery of a second language. So two difficult tasks are rolled into one, and a general failure to recognise this leads to teaching that signally falls to take the measure of the task, as argued by Winch and Gingell, 1994; see also Craig, 1996, for a brief summary of a lifetime's engagement with these issues, and Devonish, 1986, especially pp. 101–107, for discussion that puts these issues in a wider socio-political context.
3. Cf. Harold Bloom's remark that 'the West's greatest writers are subversive of all values, both ours and their own ... Reading deeply within the Canon will not make one a better or a worse person, a more useful or a more harmful citizen. The mind's dialogue with itself is not primarily a social reality' (1994, pp. 29–30).
4. For some trenchant remarks on Aristotle's project, untypical of his era, of trying to justify slavery, see Williams, 1993, ch. 5. For Hume, and various other major philosophers, making fools of themselves about Africans and native Americans, see Mills, 1997, p. 60.
5. We have hitherto said little about the implications of this aspect of an Arnoldian concern for high culture. The issues in relation to culturally plural societies have been much discussed in recent political philosophy and deserve much more extended treatment than we can give them here. The following sketch of a position is, however, offered as part of a defence of the practical implications of our position for the schools we know.
6. One of us would like to thank Shell (if a very fallible memory serves) for a documentary film he saw at school on the Greeks in which Diogenes' reply 'I am a citizen of the world' formed a part. It seemed then an eminently worthy position.
7. Miller (1998) has recently tried to show that a universalistic morality of equal respect permits us to differentiate between nationals and non-nationals, while admitting that equal concern would require of us totally unfeasible policies of redistribution. But his solution assumes what a moral justification is needed for, the division of people into national groups in the first place.
8. See Wood (1998) for a discussion of Kant's proposal for a world federation to bring about perpetual peace.
9. Cicero all but explicitly used the image of concentric circles of concern, focused on the ego, that later Stoics adopted (Nussbaum, 1997, p. 60 and note 16) and which serves to explicate the modern notion of 'self-referential altruism' in Mackie's (1977) account of ethics. In *De Officiis* Cicero insists on complex allegiances: in terms of the stringency of our obligations he concludes Book 1 by putting the immortal gods first, then our country, then our parents—these groups he had earlier identified as those which had given us the most—then our children and the rest of our family, who look to us for support, then kinsmen, fellow citizens and ultimately all mankind.
10. Nerlich's book deserves much more detailed attention in its own right and as having implications for philosophy of education than we can give it here. He aims to provide a naturalistic account of valuing and of persons, and thus invites the accusation that he has

committed the naturalistic fallacy. One way of making the point is that you only get out as much as you put in to a naturalising programme. Nerlich puts this in:

> the idea of a person...is in part the idea of an ideal or a task, something towards which we naturally aspire, all of us with some success, though never complete...To be a person, in the most minimal sense, is just to be in a natural-cultural *state*. But being in the state means *being in touch* with the ideals and aspirations, with the task...Anyone in that state will understand and even take some part in...evaluating and transforming himself—excelling what he presently is. (1989, p. 2)

The bearing of this on substantial conceptions of education, and its possible begging of key questions, should be obvious.

11. Deveaux (forthcoming) emphasises the point that cultural membership, in virtually any culture, can give people a sense of rootedness and emotional security. She is right to criticise some liberals for supposing that the main value of cultural belongingness is as a support to typically liberal virtues of autonomous choice. But as Mill said, better Socrates unhappy than a pig happy. Where is it written that education should make you feel secure? Nietzsche might have said that only an Englishman would ever have believed anything so banal.

12. If your picture of schooling is derived from Dickens, tolerance is about the last thing you will associate with it, or its cane-wielding taskmasters. Even in more enlightened, child-centred thought, there is still an oddity in linking education and tolerance. However much one stresses the child's initiative, discoveries, interest, and so on, it is clear that at the end of the day, he or she had better discover and get interested in what the rest of us (represented by the teacher and the examination system) have endorsed. Ticks and crosses are not the mechanism of tolerance.

13. Cf. Gellner's famous discussion (1989, ch. 2) of the structure of pre-industrial world views. What this implies is that our actual educational practice (what educators tolerate and what they do not) cannot be fitted into this neat distinction, nor probably any other that might be offered. Take debates about how to teach History. Whether you teach Caribbean history from the perspective of the imperialist colonisers or from that of the slaves and indentured labourers, what you teach will mix up facts and values. Some of the things we tolerate will mix up facts and values (is it not as factual as facts can get whether Haile Selassie died in 1975, yet we may not correct a Rastafarian who denies his death); some of the things we do not will also mix them up. There may be a question whether in a different world we could base toleration on a fact/value distinction—the point for now is that in this one we do not.

14. See, for example, Gutmann, 1995, who argues that the demands of a reasonable conception of civic education in effect close the gap Rawls supposes to exist between the consequences of comprehensive and political liberalism here.

15. There are, of course, practical questions about how many people must play the right game for it to survive; we can get by with some free-riders, fascists and other fanatics, or, as Gutmann (1995) stresses, with the possibility of 'partial' citizens, groups like the Amish which deliberately cut themselves off from the larger polity. But political argument can reasonably concentrate on ideals here. We would like a society as liberal as possible to persist, so let everyone be educated for it.

16. Sreenivasan (1998) has argued that relevant common ground can be discovered by parties to a (cross-cultural) dispute rather than having to be shared between them at the outset. Important, and optimistic, though this is, perhaps it amounts to little more than an acknowledgement that people can change their minds and acquire new (and better-grounded) beliefs. What was not possible for them at one time can then be possible later.

17. *Wisconsin v. Yoder*, 406 U.S. 205 (1971).

18. Leaving aside the exceptional cases where circumstances force us to come to a decision at some point, like driving on one side of the road, or adopting some form of national defence.

It is not at all obvious that anything arises for religious belief, say, parallel to our need to avoid the anarchy of driving without rules of the road.

19. The suggested way out probably imports a crude political element into the issue, since individuals are not going to be counted as representing a view unless they can point to enough fellow-believers (cf. Walzer, 1997, p. 69).

20. The qualification about moral acceptability can be important. Genocide is obviously ruled out; but so may be the influence of oligopolistic media. The State may be required to subsidise broadcasting in French or Welsh, but perhaps if no one bothers to listen its obligations have been sufficiently met.

21. As Mills and many another will point out, many thinkers have too readily assumed that people they distrusted or disparaged belonged among these exceptional cases.

7

Practical Implications

The practical implications of our thesis mainly concern the matter and manner of teaching in our secondary schools. Because this is so it is worth repeating and expanding some of the points we have made about secondary education before we begin. Because memories are short, and people often do not give history its due, it is worth reiterating that we have only had compulsory secondary education in England since 1944. The two authors of this book, for instance, were part of the *first* generation of working-class children who could expect to stay in school until, at least, middle adolescence. What this means is that we would be wise to regard our attempts, so far, at secondary education as largely experimental. It would be simply foolish to regard what we have now as a finished or final version of our ideals for such an education. If this point was not clear ten years ago it should be clear now in England after ten years of a constantly changing National Curriculum. And even the changes resulting from the imposition of such a curriculum—and those that have followed since—can be seen not as a revolutionary attempt to rethink the curriculum but rather as an attempt to enshrine what was thought good practice in 1988. As Alexander (1992) has pointed out, the National Curriculum has not changed the fact that ninety per cent of curriculum time in schools is still spent doing two things: reading and writing. And he might have noted that the writing part of this is largely concerned with writing about other writing. Whatever one thinks about the present National Curriculum—and it is a standing rebuke to British philosophers of education that they have produced no sustained work about it—it provides a mechanism for large-scale change within schools and for ways of monitoring such change. In what follows we suggest, at least by implication, that the National Curriculum is not (in its own words) as 'broad, balanced and relevant' as it might be, and that what presently goes on in schools should be seen as a temporary resting place on the way to somewhere better.

One of the obvious implications of what we have argued has to do with the breadth of the curriculum on offer. It is sometimes said that the problem with the secondary school curriculum is that it is a watered-down, public school curriculum unfitted for mass education, an idea Arnold considered and rejected in his American lecture in reply to Huxley that we discussed in Chapter 1. The idea here is that an education for gentlemen is not suitable for the grubby masses. If this suggestion concerning the birth of the modern curriculum is true then the watering down must have been radical indeed. If we take note of the categories of thought Arnold mentioned and supplement this with music and the linguistic resources he simply assumed, then the paleness of the mix is apparent. To put this in a rather different way, we belong to a culture which can boast world-class art galleries and orchestras, our twentieth-century sculptors and architects are of the first rank, the English-speaking film industry is dominant worldwide and the English-language philosophical literature is at least as rich and important as any found elsewhere; and yet we have a school system which, in general, does nothing to enable those being educated to appreciate any of these things. The teaching in our ordinary schools of music and the fine arts, for instance, is little short of scandalous. The history of art, if it is taught at all, is taught as an adjunct to learning to paint, and music is only taught seriously— again, if at all—to those who want to play an instrument. What this means is that the creativity of the very few is focused upon at the expense of the appreciation of creativity by the many.

The differences between the teaching of literature and that of art and music are instructive here. Although most schools set some time aside for 'creative writing' we suspect that any suggestion that this should be the focus of literature teaching would be greeted with incredulity. Partly, this would be based on practical doubts concerning the possibilities of producing creative writers—we might think such a goal worthwhile but we simply do not know how to achieve it. Partly, it is because learning about our literature is taken to be a good thing in and for itself. (There may even be the suspicion here that critical exposure to literature is the best method of promoting creativity.) With art and music exactly the reverse is assumed and practised. So understanding these things is completely subordinated to practising them. However, there are very different outcomes to this engagement with practice. One outcome that is not different—and again this is a suspicion—is the level of continuing interest in, say, painting or playing an instrument which survives after school days. Children may enjoy such things at school but such enjoyment does not fuel an engagement with these matters which survives leaving school. But, because of the difference in teaching in schools, those pupils who have been taught music will have critical resources which are not available to those who have been taught art. The teaching of music is typically couched in terms that are theoretically loaded. So to begin to learn to play an instrument is to begin to understand the elements of music, rhythm, melody, timbre, and so on which in turn can be used in the appreciation of the music of others. With the teaching of painting this is largely not the case. So the many hours children spend drawing and painting in schools result in the great majority of children, that is, all those that do not go on to higher education in the fine or applied arts, taking nothing with them at all from this part of school into adult life. They typically neither practise those things nor understand the practices of others. If, however, we reversed our concern in these areas, and brought the teaching of them in line with what we attempt with literature, we could at least ensure that what we are trying to do is of benefit to all the children we teach and that this benefit lasts beyond their school years. In doing so we might begin to alter the forces that currently allow the vast majority of children to leave school artistically and musically illiterate. (And it may be the case, as with literature, that a serious attempt to cultivate appreciation is the best way to also cultivate creativity and attempts to practise.)

As well as rich and resilient artistic traditions we have a varied, vibrant and important craft heritage. But just as our musical education is liable to end with the singing of sea shanties, our education in, say, cabinet-making is liable to end with the crafting of an inadequate and unwanted book-stand. Again there is no reason for this to be so. If the crafts were taken seriously in school—and seriously here means practically and theoretically seriously—we suspect that they would provide opportunities for 'sweetness and light' for many whom the school system now fails. This is not, we stress, a reversion to the Bantock or Leavis line that we have fine arts for the élite and crafts for 'the folk'. Dick Beardsmore, one of our most successful and well-rounded colleagues, combined a talent at philosophy with an equal talent for making musical instruments, and his care for 'serious' literature was paralleled by a care for 'blue grass' music. We do not know—and no one can know—what such an enlargement of the curriculum would bring, but it must offer better opportunities for everyone than the curriculum we have at the moment.

Taking such suggestions seriously means not merely a token enlargement of the curriculum so that, say, art history or music are curricular options: it means treating such additions in an academically serious way. The obvious pointer here is the way in which such subjects—and architecture, sculpture, ceramics, design and so on—are treated in higher education. This means properly funding the teaching of such things, ensuring that there are the requisite experts to teach them, monitoring the courses and ensuring that they can lead to qualifications. It means, in other words, breaking down the stultifying academic hierarchies which presently are found in our schools. At the very least, this would seem to imply that the size of secondary schools would increase to be able to accommodate such real curriculum choice. But there is little that is worrying about such a suggestion. Despite the fact that we seem to think in England that no school should go above two thousand pupils, evidence from elsewhere, for example France and the USA, seems to show that it is perfectly feasible to have much larger yet effective schools and, by doing so, achieve the economies of scale which this brings in its train. It may even be the case, given the constraints of time on any curriculum and therefore the added restraints on this one, that such an enlarged curriculum might lead to different secondary schools offering different packages of curriculum subjects, as Winch has suggested (Winch, 1996). This should not particularly worry us unless we are already worried about the type of provision offered by specialist music schools. It *might* mean that children could not, say, after fourteen specialise in physics, history, ceramics, and French, but children with such a wide range of talents and interests are rare and there *might* well be means to ensure that the odd one or two who do show such breadth are catered for. It would certainly mean more choices for children even if, in the end, each child did the same number of subjects as now. Such choice and the educational and personal advantages it would bring will, we are sure, more than compensate for any of the present benefits that are lost.

Nor should we think that such a widening and possible fragmentation of the curriculum will lead to a fragmentation of the educated public. It will, in fact, lead to an increase in such a public. It would only lead to loss if we, like MacIntyre (1987), believe that in order to have such a public we need to have a group of people who all have the same interests and exactly the same core educational experience. This may have been possible in Edinburgh during the Scottish Enlightenment, but given the diversity of human interests and the growth of specialised knowledge since that time it is no longer possible. But neither is it necessary. The notion of an educated public does not call for uniformity but rather for people to have interests—and an education to serve such interests—that diverge in parts and overlap in other parts, and a lively concern to promote each other's welfare and understanding through dialogue (cf. Mendus, 1992). The ideal of an aesthetically aware public, for instance, is not of one in which every member identically devotes time to all the arts, but rather of a group of people who understand and care about aesthetic questions and each of whose aesthetic interests focus on a few of the things on offer. No one expects even specialists such as historians to know every aspect of their specialism—'not my period' is not just a way of avoiding awkward questions—so why should anyone expect the educated person—even with regard to a particular area such as the arts—to have knowledge of all that area? Dialogue is a way of learning something new as well as of repeating a commonplace.

We want *what* is taught to change but we also want *how* it is taught to change. As we suggested in the previous chapter, it is important for the flourishing and reproduction of a liberal democracy that students come to grasp the status of the branches of study that they engage in and to explore the philosophical motivations for that kind of polity. These are probably not issues to start with, but it is not impossible to let them arise as students progress through school. A related issue concerns the dogmatism with which most school knowledge is transmitted. Although there are attempts within some presently taught subjects, for instance literature and history, to get students to engage critically with the material studied, such a practice has gone neither far nor deep enough. It seems almost entirely absent in the sciences and mathematics, where pupils are still fed 'the facts' at the expense of both intellectual curiosity and a proper understanding of the subjects involved. So, for instance, most children do leave school 'knowing' that the earth revolves around the sun but having no real understanding of the Copernican revolution which led to this 'knowledge'. But to understand this—and thus to understand why we believe what we do believe—is to approach science at a level of sophistication both in terms of its history and its theory which is hardly attempted at the moment. Another example is the teaching of Darwin's theory of evolution. Again, most children may leave school with a rudimentary notion of natural selection and an acceptance that human beings and apes evolved from a common ancestor. But too many remain impervious to such an understanding and very few acquire an appreciation of the wider significance of Darwinian views in undermining the very natural tendency to assume the need for intelligent design when contemplating the complexities of the living world.

In the teaching of mathematics the same cultural ignorance is engendered by our methods of teaching. Children may be taught the rudiments of Euclidean geometry but little attempt is made to explain why Euclid's approach has exercised such a grip upon the intellectual imagination of the West for well over two thousand years.

Elsewhere critical engagement seems to mean changing one piece of received wisdom, for example concerning the merits of the British Empire, with its opposite. This is a sop thrown to a bogus multiculturalism and is nowhere near as radical as, for instance, making real attempts to deal with women's history in a proper fashion. (And if you thought 'the boys won't like that' think about what the girls get now!) And such attempts to encourage a critical engagement with subject matter should bear in mind the points we made about multiculturalism. We urged an education that is as cosmopolitan as possible. Such an education might have certain formal features, for instance it would encourage, at least initially, teaching in the pupils' own language; it would select second languages in culturally sensitive ways, for example Punjabi or Bengali might be real options for white English children in Bradford, and it would be open with regard to whether students studied, say, European or Chinese painting. However, it might also be nuanced in ways that are different from the present situation. Let us suppose there is—as there may well be—an overwhelming case for studying English literature in English schools. Even if this is the case it does not prevent us from interpreting the category of literature in terms of language rather than geography, that is, literature written in England. But in opening up the category in this way, we also open up the possibility of presenting to students world-views which do not simply reinforce the dominant culture and which therefore may not marginalise or ignore those from outside this culture. So, for instance, to take some examples, Rudyard Kipling's *Kim*, Jean Rhys's *Wide Sargasso Sea*, Patrick White's *Voss*, J. G. Farrell's *Troubles*, Wole Soyinka's *The Interpreters* and Derek Walcott's *Omeros* are all works of literature which deal with culture clash in intelligent and sensitive ways and which therefore do not privilege a simple view of the world which may be offensive to certain students. All of these works—and there are many others—demand the serious attention which all good literature demands but, at the same time, highlight a world in which a sympathetic understanding of the cultural positions of others is a necessary condition for understanding the common world that the characters inhabit. They treat culture as something to be discovered and explored, rather than something that is simply given.

We mentioned earlier (see the final part of Chapter 3) the possibility of someone who, even if equipped to choose between better and worse in a cultural area, simply cannot be bothered to make the choice: someone for whom cultural engagement on the level we are recommending is simply too arduous. That such people are to be found is beyond doubt. It is likely that they will exist even if our approach to education is adopted. But it is important to see what is going on here. All the values that our culture offers exist, by definition, at the anthropological level of culture. Here is the totality of possibilities open to an inhabitant of this culture. (And, just as importantly, the limits of such possibilities. Some people, probably of an existentialist inclination, seem to believe that all possibilities are open. But this is nonsense; it is just impossible in the here and now to lead the life of a medieval knight or a samurai warrior.) And such possibilities leave open the choice of a life which hardly, if ever, goes beyond this cultural level: a life, for instance, devoted to family and friends, visits to the pub and an uncritical use of the mass entertainment media—in short, an unreflective life. If the attachments to personal relationships are lived in certain ways then such a life is certainly not to be sneered at. However, it is a life where the realisation of value seems unnecessarily circumscribed, given the riches which surround it. The articulation and celebration of the values of such a life—and much else—begins at the second level of culture which concerns the intellectual and artistic practices of the given culture. It is here that the culture begins to have a voice; or rather, many voices, for at this level trying to discern the message or the important messages will be like trying to make sense of conversations within the Tower of Babel. It is only when we have moved to the final level, when we have sifted sense from nonsense, gold from dross, that some clear articulation of what we are and what we are capable of becomes possible. Not to try to attend to this is to be unconcerned not merely with the body of humanity around one— both how it is now and how it has become that—but also ultimately with oneself, because what we are individually must be understood in some cultural context and it is at this level that the best understanding and elucidation of that context occurs. (And although we allowed that someone might not, through choice, partake of culture at this level, it is difficult to imagine a person who never even attempts to exercise the type of discrimination which, in the end, brings us to this level: who eats and drinks but does not care what he eats and drinks, who inhabits a place but has no concern for the look and feel of the place, who is entertained but cares not by what, who is surrounded by others not like him but has no curiosity as to the dissimilarity.) Not to be engaged at this level at all is to be culturally poor indeed. And the price of such engagement—properly understood—is education.

Although the general thrust of this book has to do with cultural value it should not be forgotten that questions of equity are also pertinent here. Arnold hoped that culture, properly understood, would bring people together and promote equality. That is our hope as well. But this will only be so if we have an education system which serves the types of ends which we have endorsed. It has been claimed by Cooper that a concern for equality and a concern for excellence cannot go together and that 'where there is a conflict, as there must be between attending to excellence and attending to an evenly spread, average improvement, there is rarely a serious question as to the preferred alternative' (1980, p. 55). But this seems wrong on at least two counts. First, if we take something like the National Health Service it seems very far from clear that most people would sacrifice an overall improvement in service for the sake of added excellence in one department. Second, it is not clear that we do in fact always have to choose between the two. Why not have both? So, for instance, the wine industry over the last few years has been filled with people trying both to produce excellent wine which can rival the best burgundy and claret, and to raise the standard of wine generally. And their efforts have met with a great deal of success on both counts—competitions for claret-type wines are now routinely won by wines from Spain and Australia, and the general quality of wine is higher than it has ever been. Cooper's notion that 'the prime concern of the lover of music or athletics is not with a general, marginal improvement in the amateur playing of string quartets, or the time clocked by run-of-the-mill runners; but with seeing the higher standards of musicianship maintained or advanced, with seeing great athletes break new barriers' (1980, p. 55) may be correct as far as it goes, but it does not fit well with a concern for education. Most of us do not believe that ultimate academic excellence is achieved within the school system (the peaks are climbed later): rather we believe that the purpose of such a system is to get as many people as possible onto a plateau from which they can see these peaks. We do not need a full-blown account of equality or equal opportunities to claim that one crucial component of such a concern, at least as far as education is concerned, is to ensure that a curriculum of high cultural value is available to all our children. Not to do so is to ensure that the flourishing of the few is bought at the expense of the many. If anyone thinks this is a desirable situation—and it is by and large the situation we have at the moment—we do not!

Bibliography

Adorno, T. (1973), *The Philosophy of Modern Music* (trans. A. Mitchell and W. Blomster) (New York, Seabury).

Adorno, T. (1976), *Introduction to the Sociology of Music* (trans. E. Ashton) (New York, Seabury).

Alexander, E. (1965), *Matthew Arnold and John Stuart Mill* (London, Routledge & Kegan Paul).

Alexander, R. (1992), *Policy and Practice in the Primary School* (London, Routledge).

Anderson, J. (1962), Classicism, in: J. Anderson, *Studies in Empirical Philosophy* (Sydney, Angus & Robertson).

Appiah, A. (1998), Cosmopolitan patriots, in: P. Cheah and B. Robbins (eds), *Cosmopolitics: Thinking and Feeling Beyond the Nation* (Minneapolis, University of Minnesota Press).

Arnold, M. (1935), *Culture and Anarchy* (J. Dover Wilson, ed.) (Cambridge, Cambridge University Press).

Bantock, G. H. (1963), *Education in an Industrial Society* (London, Faber & Faber).

Bantock, G. H. (1967), *Education, Culture and the Emotions* (London, Faber & Faber).

Bantock, G. H. (1971), Towards a theory of popular education, in: R. Hooper (ed.), *The Curriculum: Context, Design and Development* (Edinburgh, Oliver & Boyd).

Bantock, G. H. (1973), *Education in an Industrial Society* (London, Faber & Faber).

Barnett, R. (1988), Does higher education have aims? *Journal of Philosophy of Education*, 22.2, pp. 239–250.

Barrow, R. (1976), *Common Sense and the Curriculum* (London, Allen & Unwin).

Barrow, R. (1981), *The Philosophy of Schooling* (Brighton, Wheatsheaf).

Barrow, R. (1993), *Language, Intelligence and Thought* (Aldershot, Edward Elgar).

Beardsley, M. (1958), *Aesthetics* (New York, Harcourt Brace).

Beardsley, M. (1962), On the generality of critical reasons, *Journal of Philosophy*, 59.18, pp. 477–486.

Best, D. (1985), *Feeling and Reason in the Arts* (London, Allen & Unwin).

Blake, N. (1992), A position in society, an intimate constraint, *Journal of Philosophy of Education*, 26.2, pp. 271–276.

Bloom, A. (1987), *The Closing of the American Mind* (New York, Simon & Schuster).

Bloom, H. (1994), *The Western Canon: The Books and School of the Ages* (New York, Harcourt, Brace & Company).

Bloom, H. (1998), *Shakespeare: The Invention of the Human* (New York, Riverhead).

Brandon, E. P. (1979), The key of the door, *Educational Philosophy and Theory*, 11.1, pp. 23–34.

Brandon, E. P. (1980), Subjectivism and seriousness, *Philosophical Quarterly*, 30, pp. 97–107.

Brandon, E. P. (1987), *Do Teachers Care about Truth? Epistemological Issues for Education* (London, Allen & Unwin).

Brandon, E. P. (1989), Subverting common sense: textbooks and scientific theory, in: D. E. Herget (ed.), *The History and Philosophy of Science in Science Teaching: Proceedings of the First International Conference* (Tallahassee, Science Education and Department of Philosophy, Florida State University).

Brandon, E. P. (1995), *Inus* conditions and justification: a case study of the logic of Gutmann's argument for compulsory schooling, in: F. van Eemeren, R. Grootendorst, J. A. Blair and C. A. Willard (eds), *Special Fields and Cases, Proceedings of the Third ISSA Conference on Argumentation, Volume IV*, (Amsterdam, Sicsat).

Brandon, E. P. and Sirbratthie, N. (1996), Logical reasoning as a curriculum area in schools, in: D. R. Craig (ed.), *Education in the West Indies: Developments and Perspectives, 1948–1988* (Mona, Jamaica, ISER).

Casey, J. (1966), *The Language of Criticism* (London, Methuen).
Cohen, L. J. (1954), *The Principles of World Citizenship* (Oxford, Blackwell).
Collingwood, R. (1965), *The Principles of Art* (Oxford, Clarendon).
Cooper, D. (1980), *Illusions of Equality* (London, Routledge).
Cracyk, T. (1996), *Rhythm and Noise* (London, Tauris).
Craig, D. R. (1996), English language teaching: problems and prospects in the West Indies, in: D. R. Craig (ed.), *Education in the West Indies: Developments and Perspectives, 1948–1988* (Mona, Jamaica, ISER).
Dancy, J. and Sosa, E. (1992), *A Companion to Epistemology* (Oxford, Blackwell).
Dasgupta, P. (1993), *An Inquiry into Well-Being and Destitution* (Cambridge, Cambridge University Press).
Davies, S. (1991), *Definitions of Art* (Ithaca, Cornell University Press).
Dawkins, R. (1989), *The Selfish Gene* (Oxford, Oxford University Press).
Dawkins, R. (1990), *The Blind Watchmaker* (Harmondsworth, Penguin).
Dearden, R. F. (1968), *The Philosophy of Primary Education* (London, Routledge).
Dearden. R. F. (1972), Competition in education, *Proceedings of the Philosophy of Education Society of Great Britain*, 6.1, pp. 124–146.
Dennett, D. C. (1996), *Darwin's Dangerous Idea* (Harmondsworth, Penguin).
Deveaux, M. (forthcoming), Cultural pluralism from liberal perfectionist premises, *Journal of Social Philosophy*.
Devonish, H. (1986), *Language and Liberation: Creole Language Politics in the Caribbean* (London, Karia Press).
Dickie, G. (1964), The myth of the aesthetic attitude, *American Philosophical Quarterly*, 1.1, pp. 56–65.
Dickie, G. (1973), Psychical distance: in a fog at sea, *British Journal of Aesthetics*, 13.1, pp. 17–29.
Dickie, G. (1974), *Art and the Aesthetic* (Ithaca, Cornell University Press).
Dickie, G. (1997), *Introduction to Aesthetics* (Oxford, Oxford University Press).
Eliot, T. S. (1948), *Notes Towards a Definition of Culture* (London, Faber & Faber).
Elliott, R. (1986), Richard Peters: a philosopher in the older style, in: D. Cooper (ed.), *Education, Values and Mind: Essays for R. S. Peters* (London, Routledge & Kegan Paul).
Entwistle, H. (1978), *Class, Culture and Education* (London, Methuen).
Feynman, R. P., Leighton, R. B. and Sands, M. (1963), *The Feynman Lectures on Physics*, Vol. 1. (Reading MA, Addison-Wesley).
Fielding M. (1976), Against competition: in praise of a malleable analysis and the subversiveness of philosophy, *Proceedings of the Philosophy of Education Society of Great Britain*, 10, pp. 119–133.
Foucault, M. (1972), *The Archaeology of Knowledge* (trans. A. M. Sheridan Smith) (London, Tavistock).
Fry, R. (1926), *Vision and Design* (London, Chatto & Windus).
Galston, W. (1989), Civic education in the liberal state, in: N. Rosenblum (ed.) *Liberalism and the Moral Life* (Cambridge MA, Harvard University Press).
Gellner, E. (1980), *Spectacles and Predicaments* (Cambridge, Cambridge University Press).
Gellner, E. (1989), *Plough, Sword and Book: the Structure of Human History* (Chicago, University of Chicago Press).
Gellner, E. (1996), Reply to critics, in: J. A. Hall and I. Jarvie (eds), *The Social Philosophy of Ernest Gellner* (Amsterdam, Rodopi).
Gingell, J. R. (1985), Art and knowledge, *Educational Philosophy and Theory*, 17.1, pp. 10–21.
Gingell, J. R. (forthcoming), Plato's ghost: how not to defend the arts, *Westminster Studies in Education*.
Gombrich, E. (1977), *Art and Illusion* (London, Phaidon).
Goodman, N. (1976), *The Languages of Art* (Oxford, Oxford University Press).
Graham, K. (1996), Coping with the many-coloured dome: pluralism and practical reason, in: D. Archard (ed.), *Philosophy and Pluralism* (Cambridge, Cambridge University Press).

Gutmann, A. (1987), *Democratic Education* (Princeton, Princeton University Press).

Gutmann, A. (1993), The challenge of multiculturalism in political ethics, *Philosophy and Public Affairs*, 22.

Gutmann, A. (ed.) (1994), *Multiculturalism* (Princeton, Princeton University Press).

Gutmann, A. (1995), Civic education and social diversity, *Ethics*, 105, pp. 557–579.

Hampshire, S. (1954), Logic and appreciation, in: G. Elton (ed.), *Aesthetics and Language* (Oxford, Blackwell).

Harris, J. (1982), The political status of children, in: K. Graham (ed.) *Contemporary Political Philosophy: Radical Studies* (Cambridge, Cambridge University Press).

Hirst, P. (1965), Liberal education and the nature of knowledge, in: R. Archambault (ed.), *Philosophical Analysis and Education* (London, Routledge, Kegan & Paul).

Hirst, P. (1974), Morals, religion and the maintained school, in: P. Hirst, *Knowledge and the Curriculum* (London, Routledge).

Hirst, P. (1993), Education, knowledge and practices, in: R. Barrow and P. White (eds.), *Beyond Liberal Education* (London, Routledge).

Hollis, M. and Lukes, S. (eds.) (1982), *Rationality and Relativism* (Oxford, Blackwell).

Hume, D. (1951), *An Inquiry concerning the Principles of Morals* (New York, Bobbs-Merrill).

Ingram, A. (1996), Rawlsians, pluralists, and cosmopolitans, in: D. Archard (ed.) *Philosophy and Pluralism*, (Cambridge, Cambridge University Press).

Houghton, W. E. (1957), *The Victorian Frame of Mind 1830–1870* (New Haven, Yale University Press).

James, C. L. R. (1994), *Beyond a Boundary* (London, Serpent's Tail).

Kitto, H. D. E. (1956), *Form and Meaning in Drama* (London, Methuen).

Kleinig, J. (1982), *Philosophical Issues in Education* (London, Croom Helm).

Leavis, F. R. (1955), *D H Lawrence, Novelist* (London, Penguin).

Leavis, F. R. (ed.) (1968) *A Selection from Scrutiny* (Cambridge, Cambridge University Press).

Leavis, Q. D. (1932), *Fiction and the Reading Public* (London, Chatto & Windus).

Lloyd, E. A. (1997), Feyerabend, Mill, and pluralism, *Philosophy of Science* 64, 4 (Proceedings), S396–S407.

Locke, J. (1968), *Epistola de Tolerantia: A Letter on Toleration* (ed. Raymond Klibansky, trans. J. W. Gough) (Oxford, Clarendon Press).

Lukács, G. (1964), *The Meaning of Contemporary Realism* (trans. J. Mander and N. Mander). (London, Merlin).

MacIntyre, A. (1987), An educated public? in: G. Haydon (ed.), *Education and Values* (London, Institute of Education).

MacIntyre, A. (1990), *Three Rival Versions of Moral Inquiry* (London, Duckworth).

Mackenzie, J. (1998), David Carr on religious knowledge and spiritual education, *Journal of Philosophy of Education*, 32.3, pp. 409–427.

Mackie, J. L. (1977), *Ethics: Inventing Right and Wrong* (Harmondsworth: Penguin).

Martin, J. R. (1999), The wealth of cultures and the problem of generations, in: S. Tozer (ed.) *Philosophy of Education 1998* (Urbana, IL, Philosophy of Education Society).

Mellers, W. (1973), *Twilight of the Gods: The Beatles in Retrospect* (London, Faber).

Mellers, W. (1984), *A Darker Shade of Pale: A Backdrop to Bob Dylan* (London, Faber).

Mendus, S. (1992), All the king's horses and all the king's men: justifying higher education, *Journal of Philosophy of Education*, 26.2, pp. 173–182.

Mendus, S. (1995), Toleration and recognition: education in a multicultural society, *Journal of Philosophy of Education*, 29.2, pp. 191–201.

Middleton, R. (1972), *Pop Music and the Blues* (London, Gollancz).

Middleton, R. (1990), *Studying Popular Music* (Milton Keynes, Open University Press).

Miller, R. W. (1998), Cosmopolitan respect and patriotic concern, *Philosophy and Public Affairs*, 27.3, pp. 202–224.

Mills, C. W. (1997), Smadditizin', *Caribbean Quarterly* 43.2, pp. 54–68.

Nagel, T. (1987), Moral conflict and political legitimacy, *Philosophy and Public Affairs*, 16, pp. 215–240.

148   *J. Gingell and E. P. Brandon*

Nagel, T. (1991), *Equality and Partiality* (Oxford, Oxford University Press).
Nerlich, G. (1989), *Values and Valuing: Speculations on the Ethical Life of Persons* (Oxford, Clarendon Press).
Nussbaum, M. C. (1997), *Cultivating Humanity: A Classical Defense of Reform in Liberal Education* (Cambridge, MA, Harvard University Press).
O'Neill, J. (1998), *The Market: Ethics, Knowledge and Politics* (London, Routledge).
Phillips D. Z. (1970), Philosophy and religious education, *British Journal of Educational Studies*, 18.1, pp. 42–68.
Phillips, D. Z. (1976), *Religion without Explanation* (Oxford, Blackwell).
Plamenatz, J. (1960), *On Alien Rule and Self Government* (London, Longmans).
Rawls, J. (1993), *Political Liberalism* (New York, Columbia University Press).
Raz, J. (1990), Facing diversity: the case of epistemic abstinence, *Philosophy and Public Affairs*, 19, pp. 3–47.
Robbins, B. (1998), Introduction part I: actually existing cosmopolitanism, in: P. Cheah and B. Robbins (eds), *Cosmopolitics: Thinking and Feeling Beyond the Nation* (Minneapolis, University of Minnesota Press).
Russell, B. (1968), *The Autobiography of Bertrand Russell* (London, George Allen & Unwin).
Savile, A. (1982), *The Test of Time: an Essay in Philosophical Aesthetics* (Oxford, Clarendon Press).
Scruton, R. (1998), *An Intelligent Person's Guide to Modern Culture* (London, Duckworth).
Sim, S. (1992), *Art: Context and Value* (Milton Keynes, Open University Press).
Skillen, A. (1982), Freedom of speech, in: K. Graham (ed.), *Contemporary Political Philosophy: Radical Studies* (Cambridge, Cambridge University Press).
Sreenivasan, G. (1998), Interpretation and reason, *Philosophy and Public Affairs*, 27.2, pp. 142–171.
Sutherland, G. (ed.) (1973), *Matthew Arnold on Education* (Harmondsworth, Penguin).
Taylor, C. (1984), Foucault on freedom and truth, *Political Theory* 12.2, pp 152–183.
Taylor, R. (1978), *Art, An Enemy of the People* (Brighton, Harvester).
Thagard, P. (1978), Why astrology is a pseudoscience, in: P. D. Asquith and I. Hacking (eds), *PSA 1978 Volume One* (East Lansing, Philosophy of Science Association).
Thompson, F. M. L. (1988), *The Rise of Respectable Society 1830–1900* (London, Fontana).
Tolstoy, L. (1930), *What is Art?* (Oxford, Oxford University Press).
Trilling, L. (1939), *Matthew Arnold* (London, Unwin).
Trilling, L. (ed.) (1949), *The Portable Matthew Arnold* (New York, Viking).
Walzer, M. (1997), *On Toleration* (New Haven, Yale University Press).
White, J. (1973), *Towards a Compulsory Curriculum* (London, Routledge & Kegan Paul).
White, J. (1996), Education and nationality, *Journal of Philosophy of Education*, 30.3, pp. 327–343.
Williams, B. (1993), *Shame and Necessity* (Berkeley, University of California Press).
Williams, R. (1981), *Culture* (London, Fontana).
Winch, C. (1990), *Language, Ability and Educational Achievement* (London, Routledge).
Winch, C. (1996), *Quality and Education* (Oxford, Blackwell).
Winch, C. and Gingell, J.R. (1994), Dialect interference and difficulties with writing: an investigation in St. Lucian primary schools, *Language and Education*, 8.3, pp. 157–182.
Winfield, R. D. (1998), *The Just Family* (Albany, State University of New York Press).
Wittgenstein, L. (1958), *Philosophical Investigations* (Oxford, Blackwell).
Wolff, J. (1982), Aesthetic judgment and sociological analysis, Aspects No. 21, reprinted in: S. Sim (1992), *Art: Context and Value* (Milton Keynes, Open University Press).
Wolff J. (1983), *Aesthetics and the Sociology of Art* (London, Allen & Unwin).
Wood, A. W. (1998), Kant's project for perpetual peace, in: P. Cheah and B. Robbins (eds), *Cosmopolitics: Thinking and Feeling Beyond the Nation* (Minneapolis, University of Minnesota Press).

Index

Adorno, T., 73–4, 76, 78
aesthetic judgement, sociology of,
    79–84; and claims to knowledge,
    80–1, 82; and class, 81; and
    discourse theory, 80, 81;
    reductionist, 79; segregationist, 79;
    specificity, 79–80; transcendent, 79;
    truth/value, 81–2
Alexander, R., 137
anarchy, 6–7
Anderson, J., 121, 125
André, C., 32, 81
Appiah, A., 122
architecture, 71–2
aristocracy, 7
Arnold, M., 67, 85, 117, 120–1, 124, 138;
    and anarchy, 6–7; and culture, 1–6;
    and science, 43, 44
Arnoldian filter, 1, 25, 117
art, 3; conceptual/abstract, 81;
    evaluation, 53–67; good/bad
    comparisons, 60–1; history of, 138;
    limits of, 32; as popular, 69–84;
    quality in, 60; ranking in, 52–67;
    and test of time, 71
art/craft distinction, 40–2
astrology, 32–4
authorities see entities/authorities
Ayer, A. J., 85

Bantock, G. H., 4, 38, 70, 71, 72, 74, 75,
    78, 139; on class, 105–9; on high
    culture, 102–5
Barnett, R., 39
Barrow, R. S., 21, 111–16
Beardsley, M., 59, 63
Beardsmore, D., 139
beliefs/opinions, 14
the best: advantages of choosing, 20–1;
    how to choose, 49–68; identifying,
    30; logic of, 22–4
Best, D., 91, 94
Bhagavad Gita, 3
Blake, N., 110

Bloom, H., 13, 38, 39, 70
Bourdieu, P., 109–10, 130
British Banner, 3

Catholic Church, 3, 100
Chomsky, N., 110
Cicero, 68, 122
cinema, 69, 70–1, 74–5, 138
class, 105–9
cognition, 32, 43–7
Collingwood, R., 39–42
cosmology, 45
Cracyk, T., 77
craft, 40–2
critical singularism see particularism
cultural analysis, 77–84
culture: anthropological use, 17–19;
    badness of, 76–7; change in, 22,
    130–2; and choice, 67–8, 142–3;
    conceptions of, 17–21; and
    criticism, 8–9, 13; and cumulative
    build-up, 13; identifying, 24–5;
    intellectual/artistic use, 19–21;
    limitlessness of, 2–3; and literature,
    3–4; and non-standard position,
    10–12; philosophical arguments,
    9–13; and religion, 1–2, 97–9,
    101–2; and science, 4–6, 43–7; and
    social endorsement, 11; super-
    abundance of, 22; utility of, 3, 8;
    and values, 6; see also high culture;
    popular culture
Culture and Anarchy (Arnold), 1–6

Dancy, J. and Sosa, E., 39
Dasgupta, P., 46, 51–2
Dawkins, R., 11, 45
Dearden, R. F., 85, 86–7
Dennett, D. C., 45
Dickens, C., 105
Dickie, G., 64–7
Disraeli, B., 107
Dostoyevsky, Fyodor, 74
Dylan, B., 77

149

economics, 46, 56
education, 14; aims of, 22–4; American
  resistance to curriculum, 77;
  availability of, 73; and capacity to
  transform lives, 26–7; and change/
  revaluation, 29–30; and choice,
  18–21; concerns for, 105–7; for
  critical consciousness, 132–3; and
  critical engagement with subject
  matter, 141–2; as critique, 125;
  differences in teaching of art,
  literature, music, 138–9; different
  functions of, 93; and enforcement
  of boundaries, 34; and enlargement
  of curriculum, 137–8, 139–41;
  equity in, 143–4; and the familiar,
  26–7; fundamental/paradigmatic
  aspects, 27–30; and goals, 25, 26;
  and intelligence, 111, 116; liberal/
  plural, 124–30; limits to, 18;
  maximal/minimal approach to,
  126–7; multicultural context, 124,
  129–30; political goal of, 120–1;
  practical implications, 137–44; as
  process of enculturation, 17;
  psychological aspects, 106, 109;
  relevance of, 25–6; and schooling,
  21–2; and structuring of
  curriculum, 29; and subjectivism,
  55–7; and teaching of religion, 99,
  101–2; and underestimation of
  capabilities, 22–3; universal
  provision of, 111
Eliot, T. S., 69, 71, 97–8, 101
Elliott, R., 67
entities/authorities, 31–2; comparing
  between traditions, 36–8; example
  of, 32–4; identifying better or
  worse, 35–6; and limits of high
  culture, 38–43; other disciplines,
  34–5
Entwistle, H., 108
evaluation, terms of, 61–7; aesthetic, 61;
  analysis of, 63–4; disagreements
  concerning, 62; instrumentalist,
  64–7; matrix, 65–6; moral, 61;
  utility, 61–2
evolution, 45, 141

Farrell, J. G., 142
Feyerabend, P., 9, 10, 12
Fielding, M., 89, 95

filter mechanisms: Arnoldian, 1, 25;
  familiarity, 26–7; fundamentalism,
  27–30; relevance, 25–6
Forms of Knowledge, 29
Foucault, M., 80, 81
Fry, R., 81

Galston, W., 124
The Gambler (Dostoyevsky), 74
Gellner, E., 43, 68, 122
Gombrich, E., 59
Goodman, N., 59, 64
Gutman, A., 127, 130

Habermas, J., 39
Hampshire, S., 58
Hardy, T., 107
Hebraism/Hellenism, 7, 121
high culture, 38–43; argument for, 72–3;
  circumscribed view of, 104–5;
  defence of, 69–70, 97; engagement
  with, 102–4; and intelligence,
  111–16; as learned, 119; psychological barriers to, 109; and science,
  104; sociological barriers to,
  109–11; *see also* culture; popular
  culture
Hirst, P., 29, 99–100, 101
history, 3, 46–7, 77, 84, 141
Hoggart, R., 106
Homer, 3, 7, 28, 117
Houghton, W. E., 9
Hume, D., 62
Huxley, T. H., 4, 5, 85, 138

ideology, 11, 39
Ingram, A., 129
institutions, 30–1; as authoritative,
  31–43; and choosing between
  competing claims, 35–6; and cross-
  activity comparisons, 36–8; and
  cultural demarcation, 38–43; and
  justification of distinctions, 32–4;
  and truth-claims, 34–5
intelligence: and education, 111, 116;
  and the ideal, 115; linked to
  understanding/rationality, 112–15;
  and notion of fundamental importance, 115–16

James, C. L. R., 74, 85, 90–2, 95, 119
jazz, 29, 70, 71, 75–6, 77, 82–4
Joyce, J., 28

Kipling, R., 142
Kitto, H. D. E., 54
Kleinig, J., 87–8, 89, 95
knowledge, 6, 29

*Landscape with the Body of Phocion
Carried out of Athens* (Poussin),
63–4
language, 35, 41, 118
Lawrence, D. H., 105
Leavis, F. R., 4, 69, 70, 71, 78, 85, 104,
105, 139
Leavis, Q. D., 69, 70, 71, 72, 75, 78, 107
liberalism, 124–30, 131
literature, 3–4, 24–5, 102–5
Lloyd, E. A., 9, 11, 14
Locke, J., 14
Lukàcs, G., 78

MacIntyre, A., 38, 39, 140
Martin, J. R., 18, 21, 22
Marx, K., 11
Marxism, 77, 83–4, 110
mathematics, 44, 46
Mechanics' Institutes, 83–4
Mellers, W., 77
Mendus, S., 131
Middleton, R., 77
Mill, J. S., 8–13
Mills, C. W., 119, 123
Mormonism, 3
music, 24, 29, 35, 36, 67–8, 72, 138–9;
commercialism of, 75–7

Nagel, T., 126, 127, 128, 129, 132
National Curriculum, 137
Nerlich, G., 123
Nussbaum, M. C., 121–2

outsiders: and class, 117–18; dimensions
of, 117–19; and ethnicity, 118; and
gender, 118; and language, 118

particularism, 76; and comparison,
57–9; defined, 57; and morality,
57–8; and rational evaluation, 58;
truth in, 59–61; and uniqueness,
57–9; and use of general criteria, 59
Phillips, D. Z., 99–101
philosophy, 3, 9–13, 32, 34, 44–5, 46,
49–50
Plato, 4, 5, 120
pluralism, 124–30

poetry, 3, 6, 31, 32, 40, 41
Popper, K., 10
popular culture: and aesthetic judge-
ment/sociological analysis, 78–82;
and change over time, 70–1; and
class, 82–4; commercialism of,
74–7; criticism of, 70; evaluation of,
72–3; facts/values distinction, 77–8;
groundling argument, 73–4;
relationship with high culture,
69–70; and tradition, 71–2; *see also*
culture; high culture
Pound, E., 117
Poussin, N., 63–4
Puritanism, 7

rationalism, 112–14
Rawls, J., 126–7, 128–9
Raz, J., 128, 129
Real Estate Intestacy Bill, 3
religion, 1–2, 3, 6; attacks on, 98;
indifference to, 98; meaning of/
truth in, 99–101; relationship with
culture, 97–9, 101–2; teaching of,
99, 101–2; truth-claims in, 34–5
Reynolds, Joshua, 3
Rhys, J., 142
Robbins, B., 122
Russell, B., 11, 117
Ryle, G., 85

Saturday Review, 3
Savile, A., 71
science, 3, 4–6, 11, 31–2, 80, 104, 141;
centrality of, 44; cognitive, 43–7;
criticism of research in, 51–2;
development of, 44–5; history of,
50; how to choose the best, 49–52;
problems concerning, 49–52; and
pseudo-science, 32–4; teaching of,
29; and technology, 43–4; theories
of, 51; and truth, 49–50
scientific method, 45–6
Scruton, R., 70, 71, 75, 76, 78, 93–4, 99,
121
self-conception, 119–20; and choice,
120–1; cosmopolitan, 121–4; and
nationalism, 122–3; salient aspects,
120
seriousness, 67–8
Shakespeare, W., 13, 20, 28, 37, 54, 73,
74
Skillen, A., 130

Soyinka, W., 24, 77, 142
sport: and the aesthetic, 90–2, 94–5; audience for, 73–4; concern for, 85–6; cricket, 90; and education, 85, 92–5; football, 84, 108; importance of, 84–5; joys/limitations of, 92–3; morality of competitive, 86–90; problems of, 94; relationship with culture, 92; tensions within, 94
subjectivism: as counterintuitive, 54, 56; as individual, 53–4; and informed choice, 56–7; and judgements, 55; liking/thinking good dichotomy, 54; and progress, 55–6; truth/ mistakes in, 55–6
Symposium (Plato), 5

Taylor, C., 130
Taylor, R., 82–4
Thagard, P., 32–4

Tolstoy, L., 81
tradition, 24–5, 30; comparing, 36–8
Trilling, L., 1, 3, 6

Ulysses (Joyce), 28
university, 39, 103, 109

values, 6, 32, 81–2; and facts, 77–8; intrinsic/extrinsic, 40
Van Gogh, Vincent, 72, 74

Walcott, D., 142
Walzer, M., 131, 132
White, J., 122
White, P., 142
Williams, R., 78, 106
Wilson, Bishop, 1, 8
Winch, C., 140
Wittgenstein, L., 38, 112
Wolff, J., 78–82